Faith
Alone

Among Other Books by the Author

Before the Face of God. 4 vols.
Choosing My Religion
Chosen by God
Doubt and Assurance
The Glory of Christ
Grace Unknown
The Holiness of God
The Invisible Hand
Knowing Scripture
The Last Days according to Jesus
Lifeviews
The Mystery of the Holy Spirit
Not a Chance
Now, That's a Good Question!
Pleasing God
Renewing Your Mind
The Soul's Quest for God
Surprised by Suffering
Ultimate Issues
Willing to Believe

Faith
Alone

*The Evangelical Doctrine
of Justification*

R. C. Sproul

Foreword by Michael Horton

Baker Books

A Division of Baker Book House Co
Grand Rapids, Michigan 49516

Published by Baker Books
a division of Baker Book House Company
P.O. Box 6287, Grand Rapids, MI 49516-6287

Fourth printing, August 2004

Printed in the United States of America

Library of Congress Cataloging-in-Publication Data

Sproul, R. C. (Robert Charles), 1939–
    Faith alone : the evangelical doctrine of justification / R. C. Sproul; foreword by Michael Horton.
        p.   cm.
    Includes bibliographical references and indexes.
    ISBN 0-8010-5849-X
    1. Justification. 2. Justification—History of doctrines. 3. Reformed Church—Doctrines. I. Title.
BT764.2.S67 1995
234′.7′09 —dc20   95-31461

For information about all new releases available from Baker Book House, visit our web site:
                            http://www.bakerbooks.com

For information about Ligonier Ministries and the teaching ministry of R. C. Sproul, visit Ligonier's web site:
                            http://www.gospelcom.net/ligonier

To
Dr. John H. Gerstner

Contents

Figures

Foreword

While only a generation ago Roman Catholics and Protestants rarely found their way into each others' spiritual company, we now see them praying and reading Scripture together, and joining hearts, heads, and hands in the struggle against secularism. With the catholic creeds as a basis for cobelligerence, this grassroots ecumenism has produced much fruit. But it has also led to some rather naive lurches that substitute appearances of unity in the gospel for the reality. As today's political and moral struggles often form the basis for common action, the charismatic movement had already provided the tendency to relativize doctrinal distinctives and create a common basis in experience.

The evangelistic energy of evangelical Protestants has added the tendency to bury concern over the actual content of the evangel. One might say that in all of the activity, evangelism is too busy to be troubled with the evangel. In his broadly representative crusades, the Reverend Billy Graham was simply following in the footsteps of an earlier generation of Evangelicals whose missionary and evangelistic zeal encouraged them to play down doctrinal issues when founding the World Council of Churches. Reverend Graham recently reasserted his view of Roman Catholicism: "I have found that my beliefs are essentially the same as those of orthodox Roman Catholics."[1]

After decades of scurrilous caricatures and misinformation, Roman Catholics and Protestants are finally speaking to each other, and this is revealing a greater variety of viewpoints within both camps. It is also revealing (a) how little most Protestants know about their own convictions and (b) with what great ease they find the concerns raised by the Reformation to be simply irrelevant. How can this be? Has Rome's position changed? In fact it has not. The Vatican II documents as well as the new *Catechism of the Catholic Church* reinvoke the theological position of the Council of Trent, condemning the gospel of justification by an imputed righteousness. If it is not Rome that has altered its position in favor of the gospel, then it must be the other partner that has moved from its earlier position.

According to George Barna, James Hunter, and others who have surveyed the drift in evangelical conviction, Evangelicalism is redefining itself doctrinally. From its views of the self (77% of Evangelicals say that man is basically good by nature) to its views of salvation (87% insist that, in salvation, God helps those who help themselves), Evangelicalism has every reason to adopt a more sympathetic attitude toward Rome.

After all, the concerns raised by the Reformers (and by those today who believe that the gospel taught in Scripture in 1517 is still taught in Scripture in 1995) were not expressions of bigotry or party spirit. The gospel defines the church, not vice versa, they insisted, and in our day we must defend the gospel without concern for party labels. If we come to believe that the formula "justification by grace alone through faith alone because of Christ alone" is no longer adequate or foundational for the Christian message, then only spiritual pride would keep us from pursuing a common evangelistic and missionary strategy. But if that is, in fact, the teaching of Scripture, then an evangelical Protestant who obscures, denies, or fails to defend the doctrine of justification is as unfaithful to the gospel as a Roman Catholic in the same position.

Rome still believes what it did on that day in 1564 when it condemned the evangelical truth and those who maintain it. This is no surprise in a body that claims its decisions to be infallible and irreformable. But when the heirs of the Protestant Reformers no longer find this doctrine essential or central in defining the gospel, this is cause for deep sorrow and lament.

In our day it is common moral or political agendas, common experience, or common zeal and piety that define Christian unity. *Evangelical* once meant "one who embraces the catholic creeds, the formal principle of *sola Scriptura,* and the material principle of *sola fide."* It now seems to refer to a common "spirituality"— a concern for making converts, an emphasis on the experiential side of faith, and a "personal relationship with Christ." Since Mormons and other cults are increasingly adopting this "evangelical spirituality," those who fail to define unity in clear doctrinal terms may be at a loss when explaining to these zealous and deeply committed individuals why they cannot join the roundtable. Today, one can easily find theological professors at leading evangelical institutions who no longer find justification by faith alone to be true, much less necessary.[2] In much evangelical preaching, teaching, publishing, broadcasting, and evangelism, a steady diet of self-help moralism and shallow sentimentality buries whatever formal position concerning justification one might hold. For the Reformers it was not part of the gospel or the "fine print" on a piece of paper that was locked in the vault for safe-keeping. It was the "good news" and was to be proclaimed far and wide as "the power of God unto salvation," as the most important thing for a Christian to know.

In this immensely readable and relevant treatment of the great biblical announcement, R. C. Sproul has rendered the church an enormous service at a critical moment. The Reformation was not primarily concerned with the issues that Evangelicals today often think of first: the papacy, superstition, and the cult of the Virgin and the saints. First and foremost, it was a challenge to Rome's confusion over the very meaning of the gospel. How can I, a sinner, be accepted by a holy God? That was the question that sent the hearts of those who really knew themselves and their own wickedness racing. If such questions no longer disturb the conscience of the average person (including the Christian) today, it is not because God's Word has changed, but because we have been seduced by our culture into asking the wrong questions. It is not the gospel that is irrelevant, but we who, in spite of our feverish activity, proudly assert ourselves as the Red Cross Knight driving back the forces of darkness. The only torch that will enlighten our dark age is the gospel, which we now consider an impediment to our very progress.

With Martin Luther, Philipp Melanchthon, Martin Bucer, John Calvin, the heroes of the modern missionary movement, George Whitefield, Jonathan Edwards, Charles Spurgeon, and millions of evangelical brothers and sisters around the world, R. C. Sproul points us to the Atlas upon whose shoulders rests the entire Christian faith. With precision, warmth, humility, and passion, Sproul reminds us why this "good news," far from being an irrelevant historical curiosity, remains the Rock of Ages in the stormy harbor of contemporary Christianity. For those with ears to hear, his labors will not be lost.

Michael Horton
Epiphany, 1995

Does saving faith require a trust in the righteousness of Christ alone as the grounds of our justification? Or may a person have a different view of the gospel and still be a Christian?

R. C. Sproul

Light in the Darkness

In the old city of Geneva, Switzerland, there is a lovely park adjacent to the University of Geneva, close to the church where John Calvin preached and taught daily. The park contains a lasting memorial to the sixteenth-century Protestant Reformation. The central feature is a magnificent wall adorned with statues of John Calvin, John Knox, Huldrych Zwingli, Theodore Beza, and others. Chiseled into the stone are the Latin words *Post tenebras lux* (After darkness, light).

These words capture the driving force of the Reformation. The darkness referred to is the eclipse of the gospel that occurred in the late Middle Ages. A gradual darkening of the gospel reached its nadir, and the light of the New Testament doctrine of justification by faith alone was all but extinguished.

The firestorm of the Reformation was fueled by the most volatile issue ever debated in church history. The church had faced severe crises in the past, especially in the fourth and fifth centuries when the nature of Christ was at stake. The Arian heresy of the fourth century culminated in the Council of Nicea and the subsequent confession, the Nicene Creed. The fifth century witnessed the church's struggle against the monophysite and Nestorian heresies that resulted in the Council of Chalcedon and its clear declaration of the humanity and deity of Christ. Since Nicea and Chalcedon the ecumenical decisions of these councils have served as bench marks for historic Christian orthodoxy. The doctrines of the Trinity and the union of Christ's divine and human natures have since been regarded, almost universally, as essential tenets of the Christian faith.

Every generation throughout church history has seen doctrinal struggles and debates. Heresies of every conceivable sort have plagued the church and provoked fierce argument, even schism at times.

But no doctrinal dispute has ever been contested more fiercely or with such long-term consequences as the one over justification. There were other ancillary issues debated in the sixteenth century, but none so central or so heated as justification.

Historians often describe justification as the *material* cause of the Reformation. That is, it was the substantive and core issue of the debate. It was this doctrine that led to the worst rupture Christendom ever experienced and the fragmentation of the church into thousands of individual denominations.

How could a dispute over one doctrine cause so many splinters and provoke so much hostility? Was it simply a case of conflict between contentious, obstreperous, bellicose theologians, inclined to wage war over trivial matters? Was it a case of repeated misunderstandings leading to a tempest in a teapot, much ado about nothing?

We know how Martin Luther felt about the controversy. Luther called justification by faith alone "the article upon which the church stands or falls" (*articulus stantis et cadentis ecclesiae*). This strong assertion of the central importance of justification was linked to Luther's identification of justification by faith alone (*sola fide*) with the gospel. The "good news" of the New Testament includes not only an announcement of the person of Christ and his work in our behalf, but a declaration of how the benefits of Christ's work are appropriated by, in, and for the believer.

The issue of *how* justification and salvation are received became the paramount point of debate. Luther's insistence on *sola fide* was based on the conviction that the "how" of justification is integral and essential to the gospel itself. He viewed justification by faith alone as necessary and essential to the gospel and to salvation.

Since the gospel stands at the heart of Christian faith, Luther and other Reformers regarded the debate concerning justification as one involving an essential truth of Christianity, a doctrine no less essential than the Trinity or the dual natures of Christ. Without the gospel the church falls. Without the gospel the church is no longer the church.

The logic followed by the Reformers is this:

1. Justification by faith alone is essential to the gospel.
2. The gospel is essential to Christianity and to salvation.
3. The gospel is essential to a church's being a true church.
4. To reject justification by faith alone is to reject the gospel and to fall as a church.

The Reformers concluded that when Rome rejected and condemned *sola fide,* it condemned itself, in effect, and ceased to be a true church. This precipitated the creation of new communions or denominations seeking to continue biblical Christianity and to be true churches with a true gospel. They sought to rescue the gospel from the impending danger of total eclipse.

The eclipse metaphor is helpful. An eclipse of the sun does not destroy the sun. An eclipse *obscures* the light of the sun. It brings darkness where there was light. The Reformation sought to remove the eclipse so that the light of the gospel could once again shine in its full brilliance, being perceived with clarity.

That the gospel shined brilliantly in the sixteenth century is not much disputed among people who identify themselves as Evangelicals. The life of the Protestant church in the sixteenth century was not perfect, but the revival of godliness in that era is a matter of record that attests to the power of the gospel when viewed in full light.

Evangelical Distinctives

Evangelicals are called Evangelicals for a reason. That reason may change as words undergo a fluid evolution through variations of usage over time and in various cultural settings. Language changes. Words undergo sometimes radical, sometimes subtle changes in nuance and meaning. The science of lexicography is cognizant of such change. Lexicographers pay attention chiefly to two factors in the process of defining words. The first is etymology or derivation. We search for the original roots of words and their historic meanings to gain insight into present usage. Since words and their meanings can and often do change, however, it is not enough merely to examine a word's root to discover its current meaning. Philosopher Ludwig Wittgenstein, chief architect of Linguistic Analysis, argued that words must be understood in terms of their contemporary or "customary" usage.

Words are a part of the *customs* of a people. Words change their meanings as the people change. Take, for example, the word *scan*. If I tell my students to scan the textbook, what would they understand their assignment to be? Most would understand that they need only skim lightly over the material.

Historically the word *scan* meant to examine closely with fixed attention to detail. The word still carries that idea with respect to the task of air-traffic controllers. The radar scan is not a loose skimming of planes in the air. A brain scan done by a physician is likewise not a casual, "once over" viewing.

The word *scan* sounds enough like the word *skim* for people to begin confusing the two. In this confusion the term *scan* began to be used to refer to a process that means the very opposite of the word's original meaning. So what is the correct "meaning" of *scan*? Most modern lexicographers, because of the confusion in the term's contemporary usage, would probably cite both meanings.

I labor the point of language because the meaning of the word *evangelical* is not immune from such fluid development, change, and confusion. The etymology of *evangelical* is simple. It comes from the Greek word *euangelion,* or "evangel," which is the New Testament word for gospel. Historically the term *evangelical* meant literally "gospeler." It was a term used by Protestants who identified with the Reformation doctrine of justification by faith alone.

If the Reformation had two chief causes, a formal and a material cause, historic Evangelicalism has the same two causes. The formal cause of the Reformation was declared in the formula

Fig. 1.1
Doctrinal Causes of the Reformation

	Formal Cause	**Material Cause**
Latin name	*Sola Scriptura*	*Sola fide*
Translation	Scripture alone	Faith alone
Explanation	Scripture is the sole authority in doctrinal matters.	Justification is by grace alone through faith alone.

sola Scriptura, meaning that the only source of special written revelation that has the authority to bind the conscience absolutely is the Bible. The material cause was declared by the formula *sola fide,* meaning that justification is by faith alone.

Over the centuries Evangelicalism became manifest in a wide variety of forms. Manifold denominations emerged with individual doctrinal distinctives. Protestants were divided over a host of theological points, including the sacraments, church government, and worship. We have seen divergent views of soteriology and eschatology—Arminianism, Calvinism, Lutheranism, dispensationalism, and many other "isms"—all flying under the generic banner of Evangelicalism.

The term *evangelical* served as a unifying genus to capture under one heading a wide assortment of species. The two prominent doctrines that served as the cohesive forces of evangelical unity were the authority of the Bible and justification by faith alone. Though Protestants historically were divided over many issues, they were united on these two points as well as in their affirmation of the main tenets found in such ecumenical creeds as the Apostles' Creed, the Nicene Creed, and the formulas of Chalcedon.

Protestant Liberalism

The unity of Evangelicalism came under attack and began to disintegrate in the nineteenth century. The use of post-Enlightenment modernism reached a crescendo with the advent of nineteenth-century liberal theology. Nineteenth-century liberalism refers not merely to open-mindedness or anything so vague. It refers to a specific school of thought that departed systematically from historic Christianity. The writings of David Strauss, Wilhelm Wrede, Adolf Harnack, Albrecht Ritschl, Friedrich Schleiermacher, and others belong to this movement. Christianity was de-supernaturalized, the Bible as divinely inspired revelation was rejected, and the gospel was reduced to a matter of values, ethics, or social concern. The so-called Social Gospel of Walter Rauschenbusch and others shifted attention away from personal reconciliation to God via redemption from personal guilt and punishment, and toward social and cultural renewal.

The fundamentalist-modernist controversy early in the twentieth century was marked by a fierce struggle concerning the faith and mission of the church.

During this century the term *evangelical* began to be used not so much as a synonym for *Protestant* but to distinguish between liberal and conservative Protestants, between modernist and fundamentalist Protestants. The two doctrines of biblical authority and justification by faith alone were tenaciously maintained as vital elements of twentieth-century Evangelicalism.

With the increasing spread of liberalism, however, particularly through the so-called mainline denominations, the term *evangelical* began to assume an added nuance. An Evangelical was now someone who believes in personal salvation via personal faith, as distinguished from a salvation that is understood chiefly in social or cultural terms. Personal evangelism became a point of emphasis for Evangelicals. For many the word *evangelical* now began to serve as a synonym for *evangelistic*.

For several decades Evangelicals seemed suspicious about the church's involvement in social, cultural, and political matters, stressing instead the church's evangelistic mission. An unnatural split occurred between personal and social concerns in the mission of the church. Social action was now the "liberal" agenda and "personal evangelism" the conservative agenda.

The descriptive phrase "born-again Christian" came into vogue. Though historic Christianity had uniformly confessed the need of fallen sinners to be regenerated by the Holy Spirit as requisite for conversion to Christianity, some professing Christians now distinguished themselves by the term "born-again Christian."

This phrase highlights the confusion provoked by nineteenth-century liberalism with respect to the nature of Christianity and with respect to what it means to be a Christian.

Historically the phrase "born-again Christian" sounds like a kind of stuttering. It is redundant. Classical theology would argue that because regeneration is necessary to one's being a Christian, there is no such thing as an unregenerate (non-born-again) Christian. Likewise, because the rebirth in view refers to the Holy Spirit's changing a person from a sinner to a believer, there is no such thing as a born-again non-Christian.

It had been assumed that if you were a Christian then you were regenerate, or if you were regenerate then you were a Christian. Nineteenth-century liberalism and modernism changed all that. Christianity was in the process of being redefined at its core. The old assumptions no longer sufficed. Thousands, if not millions, of church members throughout Protestantism now claimed to be Christians while rejecting the categories of faith and doctrine of historic Christianity.

The second half of the twentieth century witnessed a marked change in evangelical concerns. Several factors combined to provoke these changes. First, Evangelicals began to realize that the dichotomy between personal evangelism and social concern and action was a false dichotomy. They began to understand that Evangelicalism had torn asunder what God had joined together. Historic and biblical Christianity saw personal redemption and social concern as vital ingredients of Christian faith. It was not an either/or dilemma, but a both/and mandate from God. Evangelicals became active in the social arena, demonstrating concern both for personal conversion to Christ and for societal problems.

Another factor changing the face and landscape of Evangelicalism was the meteoric rise of the charismatic movement. This movement exploded in force in the 1960s, breaking into mainline denominations and Roman Catholicism. A new "unity" was experienced, articulated in a kind of spiritual unity (we are one in the Spirit) that transcended old denominational lines. Doctrinal differences began to be played down in light of a new experience of fellowship among people from diverse ecclesiastical and theological backgrounds.

At the same time liberal theology was making a strong impact on evangelical groups, particularly with an avalanche of criticism leveled against the trustworthiness and reliability of the Bible. This onslaught of criticism created a crisis within Evangelicalism with respect to one of the two chief points of unity. The doctrine of inerrancy long upheld by Evangelicals came under attack. Harold Lindsell chronicled the debate in *The Battle for the Bible.*[1] The International Council on Biblical Inerrancy (ICBI) was formed to define and defend the conservative view. The work of ICBI during the ten years of its existence served to rally Evangelicals and shore up this sagging point of unity.

This defense of Scripture did not stop the erosion of unity among professed Evangelicals. Many individuals and institutions historically tied to Evangelicalism defected from the doctrine of inerrancy. Some opted for a watered-down view of "infallibility," while others sought a *via media* in the view of "limited inerrancy." The internecine struggle within the Southern Baptist Convention on this issue attracted the attention of the secular media.

With the deterioration of one pole of historic unity, the authority of Scripture, that left one crucial point of unity: the doctrine of justification by faith alone.

"Lordship Salvation" Controversy

In the final quarter of the twentieth century, the last bastion of evangelical unity was put under siege. The problem became manifest in two distinct areas. The first was the outbreak within the ranks of dispensationalism of the "Lordship salvation" controversy. This controversy was carried on chiefly between John MacArthur on one side and Zane Hodges and Charles Ryrie on the other. The chief question in dispute was whether a person can be saved by embracing Jesus as Savior but not as Lord. At issue were the necessary conditions or requirements for justification. The debate did not center on merit and grace, but it did (and continues to) center on faith and works.

At the heart of the issue is this question: Does saving faith *necessarily* produce the works of obedience? MacArthur insists that true saving faith must necessarily and inevitably yield works of obedience. Ryrie and Hodges insist that though faith *should* immediately produce works of obedience, it does not always do so. The "carnal Christian" is one who receives Jesus as Savior but may die without ever embracing him as Lord.[2]

MacArthur protests that this is a blatant form of antinomianism and a departure from both the biblical view of justification and the historic Protestant view. Ryrie and Hodges say MacArthur is teaching a form of neonomianism or legalism, by which works are added to faith as a necessary condition for justification. Each side argues that the other preaches a gospel different from the biblical gospel and hence a "different gospel," which places them under the anathema declared by the Apostle Paul in Galatians 1.

As this intramural debate among dispensationalists spilled over into the broader evangelical community, leaders from Lutheran and Reformed communities became involved. James Boice, Michael Horton, J. I. Packer, Rod Rosenbladt, and others entered the debate, basically siding with MacArthur. John Gerstner did the same, though he added another crucial dimension. He argued that, not only are works of obedience necessary and inevitable results of true faith, but they begin to be manifest *immediately*, being inseparable from faith.

None on the Lordship side regards works as contributing anything to the *grounds* of our justification. They insist that the works of Christ alone furnish the grounds for our justification. The issue is this: What constitutes saving faith? Is it possible for a person to have true faith and not have works?

As we will see later, the Reformers insisted that true faith necessarily, inevitably, and immediately yields the fruit of works. They argued that though justification is *by* faith alone, it is not by a faith that is alone.

Lurking behind the scenes of this debate is a crucial difference in what happens in regeneration. Is the person who exercises saving faith a changed person or not?

All who are regenerated are changed. Reformed theology views regeneration as the immediate supernatural work of the Holy Spirit that effects the change of the soul's disposition. Before regeneration the sinner is in the grips of original sin, by which he is totally disinclined toward God. He is in willing bondage to sin and has no desire for Christ. Faith is a fruit of regeneration. The believer is a changed person. He is still a sinner but is in a process of spiritual reversal that has, by the efficacious work of the Holy Spirit, already begun.

The necessity, inevitability, and immediacy of good works are linked to the work of regeneration. Also *at* and *with* justification the believer is indwelt by the Holy Spirit, and this indwelling initiates the work of sanctification.

Justification Controversy

This debate among professed Evangelicals reflects one crisis over the evangelical doctrine of justification. A second and perhaps more serious crisis has been provoked by dialogues between Roman Catholic theologians and Protestants. In an effort to reach accord over the issue that has been so divisive over the centuries, some of the sharp edges of the historic debate have been smoothed over and blunted. This may be seen in the widely publicized document that was made public in the spring of 1994. It is entitled *Evangelicals and Catholics Together: The Christian Mission in the Third Millennium (ECT).*[3]

This twenty-six-page document is the product of a consultation among Roman Catholic and evangelical representatives who began their task in September 1992. Participants in the framing of this document include (among others) Avery Dulles, George Weigel, Richard John Neuhaus, Herbert Schlossberg, Charles Colson, Richard Land, and Bishop Francis George.

ECT was signed by many representatives from both the Roman Catholic communion and the evangelical communion. Some of the noted signatories are Catholics Peter Kreeft, Keith Fournier, Michael Novak, John Cardinal O'Connor, and Carlos Sevilla, and Evangelicals Bill Bright, Os Guinness, J. I. Packer, Richard Mouw, Mark Noll, and Pat Robertson.

Our chief interest at this point is in the evangelical representatives. They included men and women from the charismatic community, the Southern Baptist Convention, Campus Crusade for Christ, Fuller Theological Seminary, Wheaton College, and Regent University. The diversity is broad, reaching far across the spectrum of contemporary Evangelicalism. Evangelicals with the stature and leadership positions of Charles Colson, Bill Bright, J. I. Packer, Os Guinness, and Pat Robertson have attracted major attention in the evangelical world.

Framers of ECT made it clear that they were participating as individuals, not as official spokespersons for the Roman Catholic Church or other denominations: "This statement cannot speak officially for our communities. It does intend to speak responsibly from our communities and to our communities."[4]

Since ECT is not an official pronouncement issued by the communities represented, it may be lightly dismissed as a mere agreement of forty or so individuals. It must be seen, however, that the document affirms not only what each of these individuals privately believes about the Christian faith, but also what they believe to be common points of faith between Roman Catholicism and Evangelicalism.

ECT is introduced by this statement:

> We are Evangelical Protestants and Roman Catholics who have been led through prayer, study, and discussion to common convictions about Christian faith and mission. . . . In this statement we address what we have discovered both about our unity and about our differences. We are aware that our experience reflects the distinctive circumstances and opportunities of Evangelicals

and Catholics living together in North America. At the same time, we believe that what we have discovered and resolved is pertinent to the relationship between Evangelicals and Catholics in other parts of the world. We therefore commend this statement to their prayerful consideration.[5]

ECT then asserts the unity of the Christian mission:

As Christ is one, so the Christian mission is one. That one mission can be and should be advanced in diverse ways. Legitimate diversity, however, should not be confused with existing divisions between Christians that obscure the one Christ and hinder the one mission. . . .

The one Christ and one mission includes many other Christians, notably the Eastern Orthodox and those Protestants not commonly identified as Evangelical.[6]

Here, without equivocation, ECT affirms that the mission of Christians is one. Diversity is acknowledged, but not at the expense of true unity. It proclaims a unity within diversity. The document implies that there are other Christians besides Catholics and Evangelicals who are included in this mission. Two groups are explicitly mentioned: Eastern Orthodox Christians and non-evangelical Protestants (at least those who are "not commonly identified as Evangelical").

This last group is vaguely defined. Does this mean that there are evangelical Protestants who are not commonly identified as Evangelicals, or does it mean that one can be both a non-Evangelical and a Christian?

This is no small question, especially in light of the modernist controversy. The issue focused on what is fundamental or essential to Christianity. Historic Evangelicalism strongly asserted that the gospel (evangel) is essential to Christianity and that belief in the gospel is necessary to be a Christian. If indeed belief in the gospel is necessary or essential to salvation, then a non-evangelical Christian is a contradiction in terms.

Though the wording here is unclear, I think it probably means that there are people who truly believe the gospel (and are evangelical in that sense) but who do not customarily identify themselves with any particular group that uses the term *evangelical* as a label.

Brothers and Sisters in Christ?

Later *ECT* partially clarifies this point: "All who accept Christ as Lord and Savior are brothers and sisters in Christ. Evangelicals and Catholics are brothers and sisters in Christ."[7] This statement seems to qualify the earlier statement about non-evangelical Protestants. If we take the statement "All who accept Christ as Lord and Savior are brothers and sisters in Christ" in a restrictive sense, it means that accepting Christ as Lord and Savior is a necessary condition for being a brother or sister in Christ. This implies that those who do not accept Christ as Lord and Savior are not Christians. *ECT* does not say this explicitly, but this statement, in context, suggests it.

As it stands, the assertion appears to be more than a statement about a necessary condition. The assertion goes beyond a necessary condition to a *sufficient condition*. The statement is what logicians call a universal affirmative proposition. It asserts that all P = Q. That is, all who do A are in the class of B. If a person truly accepts Christ as Savior and Lord, that person is a Christian.

But what is meant by "accepting" Jesus as Savior and Lord? Since the document later speaks of *faith* in Jesus Christ as Lord and Savior, we take it to mean "possessing true faith."

Certainly the Reformers of the sixteenth century would agree that true faith in Christ as Savior and Lord qualifies a person to be a Christian. (This assumes that the "faith" does not involve a denial of some essential Christian truth such as the deity of Christ. For example, Mormons and Jehovah's Witnesses claim to have faith in Jesus as Savior and Lord while denying his deity.) But given an orthodox view of the person and work of Christ, then the basic confession would suffice to be a Christian.

A burning question, however, remains: Does faith in Christ as Savior and Lord include a trust in the biblical gospel? Does saving faith require a trust in the righteousness of Christ alone as the grounds of our justification? Or may a person have a different view of the gospel and still be a Christian?

The question in the sixteenth century remains in dispute. Is justification by faith alone a necessary and essential element of the gospel? Must a church confess *sola fide* in order to be a true church?

Or can a church reject or condemn justification by faith alone and still be a true church? The Reformers certainly did not think so. Apparently the framers and signers of ECT think otherwise.

I say "apparently" because the document does not explicitly address the issue. The document can be read in at least two ways. The first is to assume that, though it does not affirm *sola fide,* Rome is still a Christian body because it does affirm (among other essential truths of Christianity) that Christ is Savior and Lord. The second is to assume that, though it *once* denied and condemned justification by faith alone, thereby condemning the gospel, Rome has since so modified her doctrine of justification that she may presently be seen as embracing the doctrine of justification by faith alone.

It seems clear that ECT assumes that Rome is a true church and that whatever doctrinal differences divide her from Evangelicalism, though they may be serious, they are not essential to true Christianity or to personal salvation.

ECT places great stress on cooperation between Roman Catholics and Evangelicals in the sphere of activity often called the arena of common grace, in other words, in matters of social justice, ethics, religious freedom, abortion, and others. Yet the call to common labor rests on a stated unity of the church's theological mission, a unity of mission with respect to special or saving grace. Here the clear assumption is that the two communions share a common faith, at least in its essential elements.

The assertion that "Evangelicals and Catholics are brothers and sisters in Christ" is problematic. It doesn't say "*all* Evangelicals and Catholics." Surely the framers of ECT would grant that not all who profess Catholicism or Evangelicalism are brothers and sisters in Christ. Rome, as clearly as Protestantism, has acknowledged that the visible church is a mixed body (*corpus per mixtum*) composed of true believers and false, wheat as well as tares.

Nor does it seem that ECT affirms merely that there are true brothers and sisters in Christ found in both communions. I know of no one who argues that there are no Christians in the Roman Catholic Church or no Christians outside of it. Rome has clearly broadened the original Cyprianic formula, *Extra ecclesiam nulla salus* (Outside the church there is no salvation). Even Trent hinted at this, and Pius IX's *allocutiones* gave more definition.[8]

The statement "Evangelicals and Catholics are brothers and sisters in Christ" assumes that these people are either "true" Catholics or "true" Evangelicals.

Richard John Neuhaus declared this affirmation to be at the core of the entire document. It is the center around which the unity of faith and mission revolves. It is this assertion, so central to ECT, that provokes serious concern about Evangelicals who endorse this document and their commitment to the essential character of justification by faith alone.

*We see justification by faith alone
as an essential of the Gospel
on which radical disagreement
continues, and we deny
the adequacy
of any version of the Gospel
that falls short at this point.*

*Resolutions for Roman Catholic
and Evangelical Dialogue*

Evangelicals and Catholics:
Together or in Dialogue?

hat does *Evangelicals and Catholics Together* say about justification? After the introduction, the first major section is titled "We *Affirm* Together." In the second paragraph of this section it says: "We affirm together that we are justified by grace through faith because of Christ. Living faith is active in love that is nothing less than the love of Christ. . . ."[1]

Here is the crucial statement of united affirmation with respect to justification. The first assertion is that justification is *by grace*. As we hope to show later in our exposition of the Roman Catholic doctrine of justification, there is nothing new here. The Roman Catholic Church has always insisted that justification is by grace. The idea that a person can be justified without grace, or that grace is at best something that merely *facilitates* justification but is not absolutely necessary for it, has consistently been repudiated by Rome. From the Synod of Carthage in its condemnation of the heretic Pelagius to the Council of Trent, Rome was clear on thiˇ

point. There is even a strong strand in Roman Catholic tradition that justification is by grace *alone* and that whatever merit the believer accrues is a "gracious" merit.

As far as the first assertion goes, that "we are justified by grace," there is no dispute between the Roman Catholic Church and Evangelicalism, nor has there been. It is probably safe to say that virtually every delegate to the Council of Trent would have affirmed that justification is by grace.

The same can be said of the next affirmation: "we are justified . . . *through faith.*" Again Rome has always insisted that faith is a necessary condition for justification. What they denied historically is that it is a *sufficient* condition. The Reformation was waged, not over the question of justification by faith, but over the issue of justification by faith *alone.* It was the *sola* of *sola fide* that was the central point of dispute.

The third affirmation is that "we are justified . . . because of Christ." What does this mean? That Christ is in some way the "cause" of justification was not at issue during the Reformation. Rome did not teach that justification was without Christ or apart from him (Rome affirmed the necessity of Christ's atonement and of his infused grace for a person to be justified). Nor did Rome consider the merit of Christ to be unnecessary. The issue was how the objective, redemptive work of Christ is subjectively appropriated by the sinner. Also crucial to the controversy was the objective *grounds* of justification. The Reformers insisted that the righteousness of Christ is the sole grounds of our justification. For Martin Luther justification by faith alone means that justification is by the righteousness of Christ alone, and his righteousness is appropriated by faith alone.

The word *alone* was a solecism on which the entire Reformation doctrine of justification was erected. The absence of the word *alone* from ECT's joint affirmation is most distressing. Had the document insisted that we are justified by grace *alone,* through faith *alone,* because of Christ *alone,* it would have gone much further in securing peace and unity between Evangelicals and Roman Catholics. The glaring absence of the word *alone* makes the statement totally inadequate as a rallying point for historic Evangelicalism.

In my initial reaction to this statement, I expressed dismay that the section on justification "retreated" to a view that ignored the Reformation and in effect trivializes the Reformation. Charles Colson took exception to that assessment and argued that no retreat was involved. Rather, he insisted, the framers of ECT were concerned to articulate a biblical view of justification that both sides could affirm. He alluded to Ephesians 2 in this regard.

The Bible certainly does declare that justification is by grace through faith because of Christ. The Bible says nothing *less* than that. However, it also says considerably *more* than that, as we will endeavor to show. Here in ECT we encounter a retreat to the *less* that ignores completely the *more*. It is a least-common-denominator type of agreement that passes over the gigantic controversy of church history regarding the *more*.

In private conversation Colson indicated that the two sides of the dialogue do not always agree on the meaning of statements in ECT. This is certainly true with respect to the joint affirmation on justification. When, for example, Rome declares that justification is because of Christ, this means something radically different from what it means to historic Evangelicalism.

If two parties agree on the wording of a statement but do not mean the same things by the words used, is the agreement a real agreement? If Evangelicals mean one thing when they say justification is through faith and Roman Catholics mean something quite different, then the agreement is not genuine.

An Analogy

Only when the parties are pressed for further clarification do the real and sharp differences between them become clear. Let me illustrate by an analogous scenario that some will undoubtedly find offensive. Suppose I met with a group of Mormon leaders to draft a joint statement entitled *Evangelicals and Mormons Together: The Christian Mission in the Third Millennium*. In this document we declare the following:

We affirm together that Christ is preexistent and preeminent. All who accept that Christ is preexistent and preeminent are brothers and sisters in Christ. Evangelicals and Mormons are brothers and sisters in Christ. Evangelicals and Mormons ought not to proselytize from each other's communions.

Suppose we then labor the point that, though we have reached (through prayer and study) significant agreement, nevertheless there are still many points of disagreement between us. These points have not been resolved and may never be resolved short of heaven. Suppose we then list ten points of ongoing dispute and disagreement as illustrative but not exhaustive. We declare that there are still other points of serious difference that are not explicitly mentioned. Our explicit list makes no mention of the deity of Christ, the cardinal issue between historic Mormonism and Evangelicalism. Indeed nowhere in our lengthy document is the deity of Christ even mentioned. How would the Evangelical community react?

Our answer to this question requires speculation. Indeed some may be delighted by the joint statement and take offense at any suggestion that the Mormon church is not a true church. Others, certainly most Evangelicals, would be outraged. They would ask: "How can you declare unity with Mormons when they deny the deity of Christ? Is not the deity of Christ an essential affirmation of biblical Christianity? Is not the deity of Christ integral to the affirmations of the great ecumenical councils that are a necessary part of catholic Christianity?" These protests would be loud and clear.

How can this scenario be analogous to the Evangelical–Roman Catholic joint statement? I said that the analogy would offend some people, especially those who wrote and signed the document. Surely they will consider the analogy unfair and unduly polemical. They will be quick to point out that whatever separates Roman Catholicism from Evangelicalism, no matter how serious it is, is not comparable to the deity of Christ.

Analogies are used for purposes of comparison. They are not identities or equivalents. When they compare apples to oranges, they break down—and they break down badly. No analogy has a one-to-one correspondence. An analogy points out a *likeness* or a *similarity* between two things.

Before I endeavor to show the likenesses in the analogy, let me first mention the dissimilarities. First, the Roman Catholic Church clearly and unambiguously affirms the deity of Christ and has consistently affirmed that this doctrine is essential to Christianity. Second, though Rome does have a second source of divine revelation in Tradition, it does not base its doctrines in the Book of Mormon. Other obvious differences need not be noted.

It is the similarity that is crucial for our discussion. The chief point of contact is that both Rome and Mormonism reject an essential truth for salvation. This statement assumes two things. One is that justification by faith alone is an essential truth for salvation, and the other is that the Roman Catholic Church rejects justification by faith alone. If these assumptions are accurate, then the point of similarity between Rome and Mormonism is that both deny an essential truth of Christianity. Some may argue that justification by faith alone is not essential or that it is not *as* essential as the deity of Christ, and therefore they take umbrage at the comparison.

It is questionable to debate degrees of essentiality. If a doctrine is essential, it is of the essence and cannot be rejected without departing from essential Christianity. Most Christians, I suppose, would agree that the nature of the gospel is essential to Christianity, but in all probability most would as readily agree to this as would agree that the deity of Christ is essential. That is why I stated the argument in conditional terms. I said that *if* justification by faith alone is essential for salvation and *if* Rome rejects justification by faith alone, then the conclusion follows by resistless logic that Rome rejects an essential truth of Christianity.

When I use the word *if* here, I do it for the sake of the present argument. In my mind there is no *if* about it. I am convinced, as were the Reformers, that justification by faith alone is essential to the gospel and that Rome clearly rejects it.

Again, *if* these assumptions are correct, then the point of the analogy stands: both documents declare a unity between two communions that differ on essential truths of the Christian faith.

The second point of similarity is that both documents appeal to Scripture as the basis for unity. As *ECT* appeals to Scripture to affirm that justification is by grace through faith because of Christ, so my mythical document appeals to Scripture to affirm jointly with Mormons that Christ is preexistent and preeminent. The Bible clearly teaches the preexistence and preeminence of Christ. It teaches nothing less. But it also teaches considerably more.

The third point of similarity is that both documents remain silent about the most crucial point of debate between the two parties. Just as *ECT* ignores the issue of justification by faith alone, so my mythical document is totally silent about the deity of Christ. The point is obvious. How could anyone draft a statement affirming unity between Evangelicals and Mormons without addressing the most critical point of dispute between them? In light of the crucial character of the deity of Christ, such a statement of unity would be a theological farce.

The fourth point of similarity in the analogy is that, though both sides agree to a common affirmation about an important matter, they understand the meaning of the joint statement in radically different terms. Just as Evangelicals historically have differed sharply from Rome on what the statement "by grace, through faith, and because of Christ" means, so Evangelicals differ radically from Mormons on the meaning of Christ's preexistence and preeminence. Orthodox Christianity believes Christ is preexistent to the world because he is eternal. Mormonism believes Christ is preexistent to the world because God created him before the world was made. Likewise orthodox Christianity believes Christ is preeminent because he is very God of very God. Mormonism believes Christ is preeminent because he is the most exalted of all creatures. These differences are of the very essence of Christianity.

The central point of my analogy of the mythical document is that the statement of unity ignores the most crucial point at issue between two communions, both of which claim to be authentic Christian bodies.

The Missing Doctrine

Does *ECT* ignore the crucial issue of justification by faith alone? We have already noted that the document nowhere mentions the doctrine explicitly. It does not appear in the positive affirmation concerning justification. It is not in the representative list of ongoing points of difference. In the third section of the document we read this:

> We note some of the differences and disagreements that must be addressed more fully and candidly in order to strengthen between us a relationship of trust in obedience to truth. Among points of difference in doctrine, worship, practice, and piety that are frequently thought to divide us are these:
>
> - The church as an integral part of the Gospel or the church as a communal consequence of the Gospel.
> - The church as visible communion or invisible fellowship of true believers.
> - The sole authority of Scripture (*sola scriptura*) or Scripture as authoritatively interpreted in the church.
> - The "soul freedom" of the individual Christian or the Magisterium (teaching authority) of the community.
> - The church as local congregation or universal communion.
> - Ministry ordered in apostolic succession or the priesthood of all believers.
> - Sacraments and ordinances as symbols of grace or means of grace.
> - The Lord's Supper as eucharistic sacrifice or memorial meal.
> - Remembrance of Mary and the saints or devotion to Mary and the saints.
> - Baptism as sacrament of regeneration or testimony to regeneration.[2]

This list nowhere mentions justification by faith alone. Indeed justification is not included at all (unless it is hinted at in the veiled issue of sacerdotalism).

These points are further qualified in *ECT:* "This account of differences is by no means complete. Nor is the disparity between

positions always so sharp as to warrant the 'or' in the above formulations."[3]

The document repeatedly qualifies this list by referring to other
points of disagreement that are not explicitly mentioned. On page
8 we read: "We do not deny but clearly assert that there are disagreements between us."[4] On page 9 we read: "We do not pre-
sume to suggest that we can resolve the deep and long-standing
differences between Evangelicals and Catholics."[5]

Whatever is meant by these references to "disagreements" and
"differences," we must conclude that somehow *sola fide* is
included among them, though never explicitly mentioned.

The omission of any explicit reference to *sola fide* raises a per-
plexing question. Did the framers and signers of *ECT* assume that
either (1) *sola fide* is not an *essential* issue between Roman
Catholics and Evangelicals or (2) the historic debate has been
resolved by recent developments in Rome?

When *ECT* was first released, I corresponded with some of the
Evangelicals who had signed it. I asked each person a specific
question: "Do you believe that *sola fide* is an essential and necessary element of the gospel?" Though I received replies from
most of them, none answered my question explicitly. As a result
that question still haunts me. I do not know for sure what is
believed by *ECT*'s framers and signers except for those who later
signed the *Resolutions for Roman Catholic and Evangelical Dialogue*[6] (drafted by Michael Horton and revised by J. I. Packer).

Since *ECT* is silent with respect to *sola fide*, I drew the inference
that the framers did not regard the doctrine to be essential to
Christianity. Because Rome has rejected *sola fide* and the document concludes that Evangelicals and Catholics are brothers and
sisters in Christ, it seems to me that whatever differences remain
between Evangelicals and Roman Catholics, these differences are
not essential. If they were essential, then the two communions
could not recognize each other as legitimate Christian bodies.
There cannot be a common mission of faith between a Christian
communion and a non-Christian communion.

I believe the inference that the framers do not regard *sola fide*
as essential to the gospel is a necessary inference unless they are
convinced the long-standing deep divide over *sola fide* has been

resolved. It is not enough that the issue be ameliorated; it must be resolved. *Sola fide* either is or is not essential to the gospel. No *tertium quid* is possible. If it is essential to the gospel and one communion or the other denies it, then one of the two communions denies or rejects an essential of the gospel.

Agreement between Rome and Evangelicals can be reached in several ways. One is for Evangelicals to abandon their historic position of *sola fide*. A second is for Rome to adopt *sola fide* as its official doctrine. The third is for agreement to be reached that *sola fide* is not essential to the gospel. I contend that none of these has occurred.

A Betrayal of the Gospel

If *sola fide* is essential to the gospel and to Christianity and *if* Rome has not adopted *sola fide* as its doctrinal position, then ECT seriously betrays the gospel.

Surely the Evangelicals who signed the document did not intend to betray the gospel. It is clear that their motivation was to affirm the gospel. In the fourth section of ECT they declare:

> The cause of Christ is the cause and mission of the church, which is, first of all, to proclaim the Good News that "God was in Christ reconciling the world to himself, not counting their trespasses against them, and entrusting to us the message of reconciliation" (2 Corinthians 5). To proclaim this Gospel and to sustain the community of faith, worship, and discipleship that is gathered by this Gospel is the first and chief responsibility of the church. All other tasks and responsibilities of the church are derived from and directed toward the mission of the Gospel.[7]

What follows this statement is a lengthy exposition of the societal and ethical areas of common cause. It is noteworthy that ECT does not isolate these issues from the chief mission of proclaiming the gospel.

Clearly the intent of ECT is to declare a common mission that first and foremost requires the proclamation of the gospel. No one intends to compromise, negotiate, betray, or undermine the gospel.

But the glaring problem remains, What is the gospel? The Apostle Paul warned the Galatians against preaching any other gospel than the apostolic gospel. He declared that if anyone, even an angel from heaven, preached any other gospel, then that person should be accursed. Later we will give a more detailed analysis of that warning. For now let it suffice that the apostle recognized only one gospel. This apostolic gospel either did or did not include *sola fide* as a necessary and essential element.

Again if Rome denies *sola fide* and if *sola fide* is an essential element of the gospel, then no matter what the authors' intentions, ECT involves a tacit betrayal of that gospel.

The Reformers viewed justification as being forensic, resting on God's judicial declaration that the sinner is counted as just or righteous by virtue of the imputation of the righteousness of Christ. To be declared just on the sole grounds of the imputation of Christ's righteousness was to them the very essence of the gospel.

ECT nowhere mentions forensic justification or the concept of imputation, the fiery issues of the Reformation. Is a doctrine that denies the forensic character of justification properly called the gospel? If justification rests in part or in toto on anything other than the imputed righteousness of Christ, may it properly be called the biblical gospel?

Resolutions for Dialogue

These are the chief concerns addressed by the Horton-Packer document entitled *Resolutions for Roman Catholic and Evangelical Dialogue*. Though this document contains seven distinct affirmations, we will reproduce only four of them here.

The second affirmation of *Resolutions* declares this:

The doctrine of justification by grace alone through faith alone because of Christ alone has since the Reformation been acknowledged by mainstream Protestants as "the article by which the church stands or falls," and the tenet that distinguishes a true from a false church. While affirming an indissoluble bond between justification and sanctification, this doctrine insists that justification itself is God's present forensic declaration of pardon and acceptance, and that the righteousness required for this declaration is neither attained by human effort nor infused or worked internally by God in the human soul, but is the righteousness of Jesus Christ imputed to those who believe. The Council of Trent anathematized those who embrace this doctrine, and all subsequent magisterial declarations, including those of the Second Vatican Council, continue to bind Roman Catholics to the conviction that this Gospel of free justification by faith alone, apart from works, and the assurance of salvation that springs from it, is not consonant with Roman Catholic teaching. While gladly noting in modern Roman Catholic exposition a growing emphasis on Christ and the biblical promises as objects of faith and trust, *we see justification by faith alone as an essential of the Gospel on which radical disagreement continues, and we deny the adequacy of any version of the Gospel that falls short at this point.*[8]

This article emphasizes the word *alone* as it modifies or qualifies *grace, faith,* and *Christ.* It reaffirms Luther's evaluation that *sola fide* is the article by which the church stands or falls. It confesses that this tenet distinguishes between a true and a false church.

Next the article clearly affirms the forensic character of justification, pointing to the imputation of Christ's righteousness as that which meets the requirement necessary for justification.

Most important is the unambiguous assertion that *sola fide* is an "essential" of the gospel. It states that "radical" disagreement continues. *Radical* comes from the Latin *radix,* which means "root." The difference between *sola fide* and the Roman Catholic doctrine of justification lies at the very root of the matter. Finally, article 2 denies the "adequacy" of any version of the gospel that falls short at this turn.

Here *Resolutions* reflects the authors' stated desire to debate the issue in an irenic spirit. To indicate that the Roman view is "inadequate" or that it "falls short" is a gentle criticism. In my estimation it is too gentle. One could construe this statement to mean that, though it has shortcomings and is less than adequate, the Roman "version of the gospel" is still just that, a "version of the gospel." The New Testament makes it clear that there is only one gospel. An "inadequate" gospel is not the gospel. A "gospel" that falls short of its essence is not a true gospel and must be vigorously rejected.

The next article we will examine, article 6, states the following:

> We affirm that individual Roman Catholics who for whatever reason do not self-consciously assent to the precise definitions of the Roman Catholic Magisterium regarding justification, the sole mediation of Christ, the relation between faith and the sacraments, the divine monergism of the new birth, and similar matters of evangelical conviction, but who think and speak evangelically about these things, are indeed our brothers and sisters in Christ, despite Rome's official position. We perceive that the Roman Catholic Church contains many such believers. We deny, however, that in its present confession it is an acceptable Christian communion, let alone being the mother of all the faithful to whom every believer needs to be related.[9]

Here *Resolutions* openly avows that there are many Christians within the Roman Catholic communion. This does not endorse or recognize Rome officially as a true or authentic church. Rome's official repudiation of *sola fide* disqualifies her as an acceptable Christian communion. Yet members of Rome who do embrace *sola fide* are brothers and sisters in Christ. This is declared to be the case "despite Rome's official position."

We are aware that membership in a particular religious body does not necessarily require agreement with all of that body's expressed theological positions. Protestant communions affirm that the official confessions stating their doctrines are open to correction, reformation, and change. These confessions are not infallible or beyond reforming. Since Rome claims infallibility for its teaching office, believers who affirm justification by faith alone and stay within the Roman Catholic Church must differ not only with their church's view of justification but also with their church's view of its infallible teaching office. I am convinced that any Christian who belongs to a communion that rejects an essential truth of Christianity is duty-bound to leave that communion and break fellowship with it. Obviously those Evangelicals who stay in Rome either disagree with that assessment or do not believe their communion's defection from the gospel is a serious one.

The flap over *ECT* is over this very point: the recognition of Rome as a true church despite its view of justification. Leading "Evangelicals" such as Os Guinness, Charles Colson, Bill Bright, and Mark Noll obviously must not believe Rome is disqualified as a true church. Those who signed the Horton-Packer document must think otherwise. The signers of that document include such leaders as James Boice, David Wells, Roger Nicole, John Armstrong, Edmund Clowney, Tom Nettles, Robert Godfrey, Robert Preus, and John Warwick Montgomery. Especially noteworthy is the number of faculty members serving in such seminaries as Westminster, Trinity, Gordon-Conwell, and Reformed.

There is confusion regarding the position of J. I. Packer, since he signed both documents. He has explained this by emphasizing that the value of *ECT* rests in its desire to galvanize both groups to work together as cobelligerents in the arena of common grace. Packer views that document as a rallying call for common struggle against the evils of secularism, not as a formal statement of doctrinal unity.

Evangelical Disunity

The unity that was once tacitly assumed to exist among professed Evangelicals does not in fact exist. One repercussion of *ECT* is that it has revealed a serious disunity among Evangelicals on the question of justification and the nature of Rome.

Charles Colson is convinced that Evangelicals who participated in drafting *ECT* gave nothing away and did not compromise the gospel. Others, including myself, believe that the document seriously compromises the gospel and negotiates away the very heart of historical Evangelicalism.

I may be wrong. Colson may be wrong. One thing is absolutely certain: there is serious disagreement about this question.

Prison Fellowship clearly affirms *sola fide* in its doctrinal statement. How does this square with its president's signing of ECT? Likewise I wonder if Campus Crusade affirms justification by faith alone as an essential element of the gospel.

A shadow is now cast not merely over evangelical organizations and institutions, but over the doctrine of justification itself. There is confusion over the doctrine with respect to both its content and its essential character. When ECT was announced in the press, Timothy George was quoted in *Christianity Today* as saying that the Reformation doctrine of *sola fide* was "duly affirmed" by the document. An editorial in the *Southern Florida Baptist* magazine likewise declared that the document affirmed the Reformation doctrine of justification.

I found such statements surprising when ECT never once even mentions justification by faith alone nor affirms it in any way.

The light of the Reformation is waning. The historic view is in danger of being eclipsed by the current confusion about it. Perhaps the best thing that will result from ECT is that the controversy it provokes may result in a fresh study of justification and in a reaffirmation of the Reformation. Controversies usually generate much heat, but out of that heat the light often emerges.

The light of the biblical gospel is more important than historical alliances. It is far more important than any manifestation of cobelligerency on social and political matters. The gospel is the veritable power of God to save.

We do not live in the sixteenth century. The problems we face are in many ways different from those faced by Christians in that era. Surely the fierce opposition against the church today makes it desirable for Christians to join together whenever possible. The call to unity was no idle prayer by our Lord. The goal of Christian unity is compelling, in every age and in every generation. Yet the gospel does not change. What was the power of God unto salvation in the first century is still the power of God unto salvation today. Our unity is to be rooted in one Lord, one faith, and one baptism. This is genuine unity that can never be achieved if we hold to different faiths.

The purpose of *Faith Alone* is to explore the doctrine of justification in its biblical and historical context.

*They preach human folly
who pretend that
as soon as money
in the coffer rings,
a soul from purgatory springs.*

Martin Luther

3

Watershed at Worms

April 17, 1521: On this day in history the Augustinian monk Martin Luther, already embroiled in controversy, under the condemnation of the papal bull *Exsurge Domine* issued by Leo X,[1] stood before the imperial Diet of Worms. The newly elected Holy Roman Emperor, Charles V, had summoned Luther to this place for a hearing regarding his teachings. Such a hearing had been urged by Luther's protector, Elector Frederick the Wise of Saxony.

Luther, in danger and in fear of his life, made the journey bearing letters of safe conduct issued by the emperor and various German princes. The trip, undertaken in a covered wagon, required fifteen days.[2] Luther was accompanied by a few friends—colleagues from the university, a student, and a fellow monk.[3] Luther arrived at Worms on April 16, a scene described by Gordon Rupp: "On the morning of April 16th, a trumpet sounded and the crowd pressed towards the gates . . . as a proud cavalcade of nobles and knights clattered by; at the end the little covered wagon swaying round the bend. The crowd stared and murmured their fill at the Black monk who stared back with quick, shining eyes."[4]

Luther came to Worms in fear and trembling. There was boldness and courage to be sure. But it was a courage required by the piercing fear that haunted the man. Rupp writes:

> It was the climax of months of inner struggle. For Luther was no loud-mouthed fanatic with a hide like a rhinoceros. The taunts flung at him by his enemies found an echo in his own tormented self-questioning. "How often has my trembling heart palpitated— are you alone the wise one? Are all the others in error? Have so many centuries walked in ignorance? What if it should be you who err, and drag so many with you into error, to be eternally damned?"[5]

Luther spoke openly to his friends Philipp Melanchthon and Georg Spalatin about his struggle: "'I shall enter Worms under my Captain, Christ, despite the gates of Hell,' he told Philipp, and 'I come, my Spalatin, and we shall enter Worms despite the gates of Hell, and the powers of the air.'"[6]

Luther later recalled the day: ". . . the condemnation had already been published in every town, so that the herald himself asked me whether I still intended to go to Worms. Though, in truth I was physically afraid and trembling, I replied to him: 'I will repair thither, though I should find there as many devils as there are tiles on the house tops.'"[7]

Two Hearings at Worms

The first hearing at Worms took place on April 17, the day after Luther's arrival. It was held in the "Bishop's Court": "There, in the presence of his imperial majesty, the electors and princes—all the estates of the empire—Johann von der Ecken, chancellor of the bishop of Trier, asked Luther two questions: 'Do you, Martin Luther, recognize the books published under your name as your own? Are you prepared to recant what you have written in these books?'"[8]

For Luther the afternoon of April 17 had not gone well. He was forced to wait for two hours outside the court before being called to the hearing. After he entered, he soon discovered there would be no "hearing," no opportunity for debate. The emperor and the papal legate Hieronymus Aleander refused to believe that one young man could produce so many volumes in so short a time.

Luther's lawyer, Hieronymus Schurff, objected to the first question and demanded that the titles of the books be named.[9]

With respect to the question of recantation, the audience waited for Luther's reply: ". . . as the audience chamber focused on him in a moment of hushed silence, Luther's voice sounded faint and abashed. He did acknowledge his writings, he said, but since they involved faith, salvation and the Word of God, he asked time to consider."[10]

That evening, alone in his room, Luther poured out his heart in prayer. His prayer reveals the soul of a terrified man prostrate before his God, desperately seeking assurance and courage to do the right thing. It was Luther's private Gethsemane:

O almighty and everlasting God! How terrible is this world! Behold it openeth its mouth to swallow me up, and I have so little trust in thee! How weak is the flesh and how powerful is Satan! If it is in the strength of this world only that I must put my trust, all is over! My last hour is come, my condemnation has been pronounced.

O God! O God! O God! Do thou help me against all the wisdom of the world! Do this; thou shouldst do this; thou alone, for this is not my work but thine! I have nothing to do here, nothing to contend for with these great ones of the world! I should desire to see my days flow on peaceful and happy. But the cause is thine, and it is a righteous and eternal cause, O Lord! Help me! Faithful and unchangeable God! In no man do I place my trust. It would be vain—all that is of man is uncertain, all that cometh of man fails.

O God! My God, hearest thou me not? My God, art thou dead? No! No, thou canst not die! Thou hidest thyself only. Thou hast chosen me for this work. I know it well! Act then, O God, stand at my side, for the sake of thy well-beloved Son, Jesus Christ, who is my defense, my shield, and my strong tower.

Lord, where stayest thou? O my God, where art thou? Come, come! I am ready to lay down my life for thy truth, patient as a lamb. For it is the cause of justice—it is thine! O I will never separate myself from thee, neither now nor through eternity! And though the world may be filled with devils, though my body, which is still the work of thy hands, should be slain, be stretched upon the pavement, be cut in pieces, reduced to ashes—my soul is thine! Yes, I have the assurance of thy word. My soul belongs to thee! It shall abide forever with thee. Amen.

O God! Help me! Amen.[11]

On the morrow Luther appeared once more before the diet. This hearing was held in a larger and even more crowded auditorium. The hall was dark, illumined only by smoking flares. Johann Eck began with a stern rebuke:

His Imperial Majesty has assigned this time to you, Martin Luther, to answer for the books which you yesterday openly acknowledged to be yours. You asked time to deliberate on the question whether you would take back part of what you had said or would stand by all of it. You did not deserve this respite, which has now come to an end, for you knew long before why you were summoned. And every one—especially a professor of theology—ought to be so certain of his faith that whenever questioned about it he can give a sure and positive answer. Now at last reply to the demand of his Majesty, whose clemency you have experienced in obtaining time to deliberate. Do you wish to defend all of your books or to retract part of them?[12]

Luther responded with a lengthy speech in which he divided his writings into various classes and directly recanted nothing. Eck responded with annoyed irritation:

Luther, you have not answered to the point. You ought not to call in question what has been decided and condemned by councils. Therefore I beg you to give a simple, unsophisticated answer without horns (*non cornutum*). Will you recant or not?[13]

To this direct mandate Luther gave his historic reply:

Since your Majesty and your Lordships ask for a plain answer, I will give you one without either horns or teeth. Unless I am convicted by Scripture or by right reason (for I trust neither in popes nor in councils, since they have often erred and contradicted themselves)—unless I am thus convinced, I am bound by the texts of the Bible, my conscience is captive to the Word of God, I neither can nor will recant anything, since it is neither right nor safe to act against conscience. God help me. Amen.[14]

The die was cast. The watershed moment of Christian history had been reached. Emperor Charles V was furious. "The Emperor cut short the audience with a quick, imperious gesture, and there was an ugly moment of confusion when some imagined Luther was put under arrest," Rupp reports. "But he reached safely the friendly faces, and as they pressed out into the hall Luther stretched out his arm like a victorious warrior, and his voice sounded clear above the din—'I am through! I am through!'"[15]

On May 8 Charles V drafted an edict, and on May 26 he signed it. In this edict he referred to Luther's doctrine as a "cesspool of heresies." The day after Luther's hearing he gave a speech in which he declared: "A single monk, led astray by private judgment, has set himself against the faith held by all Christians for more than a thousand years. He believes that all Christians up to now have erred. Therefore, I have resolved to stake upon this cause all my dominions, my friends, my body and blood, my life and soul."[16]

The emperor was as determined as Luther to fight the issue to the finish. He went on to say: "After Luther's stiff-necked reply in my presence yesterday, I am now sorry that I have so long delayed moving against him and his false doctrines. I have made up my mind never again, under any circumstances, to listen to him. Under protection of his safe-conduct he shall be escorted to his home. But he is forbidden to preach and to seduce men with his evil beliefs and incite them to rebellion."[17]

Causes of the Firestorm

The Diet of Worms did not occur *de novo* from the head of Zeus. Nor was it provoked by a solitary event. The events leading up to and culminating in this watershed moment were varied and multiple. There was a confluence, a convergence of political, economic, spiritual, and theological streams to form this rushing river.

Martin Luther did not set out to be a radical reformer. Roland Bainton, perhaps Luther's most famous biographer, borrowed an expression from Karl Barth to explain what happened: "[Luther] was like a man climbing in the darkness a winding staircase in the steeple of an ancient cathedral. In the blackness he reached out to steady himself, and his hand laid hold of a rope. He was startled to hear the clanging of a bell."[18]

In his early monastic life Luther was anything but spiritually steady. It is a matter of record that Luther suffered uncommon anguish as he sought desperately for peace in his soul. In 1505 he decided suddenly to enter monastic life after he was knocked from his horse by a bolt of lightning. In terror he cried out, "St. Anne help me! I will become a monk."[19]

Five years later Luther suffered another spiritual crisis. His personal odyssey of faith reached its nadir during his pilgrimage to Rome. There he was shaken to the depths by the unbridled corruption he witnessed among the Roman clergy. It is reported that after he reached the top of the stairs of the *Scala Sancta* on his knees, he whispered to himself, "Who knows whether all this is true?"[20] Of this experience he said that he went to Rome with onions and came back with garlic.[21]

In 1512 Luther received his Doctor of Theology degree and began lecturing at Wittenberg on biblical literature and theology. From 1513 to 1515 he lectured on the Psalms; from 1515 to 1516, on Romans. After Romans he lectured on Galatians, Hebrews, and Titus. His preparation for these lectures was formative for his thinking on justification.

Luther's famous "tower experience" is chronicled by Bainton:

> I greatly longed to understand Paul's Epistle to the Romans and nothing stood in the way but that one expression, "the justice of God," because I took it to mean that justice whereby God is just and deals justly in punishing the unjust. My situation was that, although an impeccable monk, I stood before God as a sinner troubled in conscience, and I had no confidence that my merit would

assuage him. Therefore I did not love a just and angry God, but rather hated and murmured against him. Yet I clung to the dear Paul and had a great yearning to know what he meant.

Night and day I pondered until I saw the connection between the justice of God and the statement that "the just shall live by his faith." Then I grasped that the justice of God is that righteousness by which through grace and sheer mercy God justifies us through faith. Thereupon I felt myself to be reborn and to have gone through open doors into paradise. The whole of Scripture took on a new meaning, and whereas before the "justice of God" had filled me with hate, now it became to me inexpressibly sweet in greater love. This passage of Paul became to me a gate to heaven. . . .[22]

This awakening to the gospel was possibly triggered by Luther's reading of an obscure comment of St. Augustine, who explained that the divine righteousness of which Paul speaks is not the righteousness by which God himself is righteous, but the righteousness that God gives to us by faith.

The Indulgence Controversy

Luther's spiritual awakening collided head-on with the preaching and actions of Johann Tetzel in the spring of 1517.

The matter of indulgences was linked to justification by virtue of its connection to the sacrament of penance. This sacrament was defined by Rome as the second plank of justification for those who had made shipwreck of their souls. Penance is restorative. The initial grace of justification is communicated by baptism. That grace is lost when one commits mortal sin. Mortal sin, unlike venial sin, destroys or "kills" justifying grace.

The sacrament of penance has three constituent parts: contrition, confession, and satisfaction. Indulgence was primarily the commutation of the act of satisfaction. Rupp observes:

In 1300 Boniface VIII issued a Jubilee Indulgence to all who visited the tombs of the Apostles on fifteen successive days: originally limited to one-hundred-year intervals, the Jubilees became more and more frequent as papal financial difficulties deepened.

Fig. 3.1
Key Popes and Papal Declarations

Boniface VIII	1294–1303		
Clement VI	1342–52	*Unigenitus Dei Filius*	1343
Sixtus IV	1471–84		
Julius II	1503–13		
Leo X	1513–21	*Exsurge Domine*	1520
Pius IV	1559–65		
Pius IX	1846–78		
Pius XII	1939–58	*Mystici corporis*	1943
		Humani generis	1950

The practice found theoretical justification in the doctrine of the Treasure of Merits of Christ and the Saints, expounded by Alexander of Hales (*Summa,* IV, qu. 83) and confirmed in the Bull *Unigenitus* of Clement VI, 1343, which includes the statement that Christ "acquired a treasure for the Church militant." In 1476 Pope Sixtus IV extended the scope of an Indulgence to the souls in purgatory. By the beginning of the sixteenth century, Indulgences had become a holy business (*sacrum negotium*) so complex as to demand the superintendence of the Banking House of Fugger.[23]

The corruption surrounding the sale of indulgences in the sixteenth century was prompted by economic problems and a financial crisis affecting both the Vatican and the Hohenzollern Prince Albert of Brandenburg. Albert, though underage for the office, was bishop of Magdeburg and Halberstadt. Despite the fact that a plurality of bishoprics was illegal, he also sought confirmation as archbishop of Mainz. In effect the new bishopric was sold to Albert in a crass manifestation of simony.

Harold Grimm reports on the arrangement:

The representatives of Albert and the cathedral chapter of Mainz, having learned that they could obtain the dispensation for 10,000 ducats—in addition to the customary fee of 12,300 ducats—offered the papal official in charge of such matters a smaller amount. The official, a good bargainer, suggested that 12,000 ducats would be a more appropriate amount, for it corresponded to the number of apostles. Albert's spokesmen countered with the suggestion that since there were but seven deadly sins, 7,000 ducats would be more appropriate. The Germans finally agreed to pay 10,000 ducats, corresponding to the Ten Commandments, after they had learned that the archbishop would be reimbursed from the proceeds obtained from the sale of the plenary indulgences. . . . [24]

Albert borrowed money from the Fugger bankers to close his deal with Pope Leo X, who also faced a financial crisis. A plenary indulgence had been inaugurated by Pope Julius II to raise funds for rebuilding the basilica of St. Peter's. This indulgence was revived by Leo X, his successor. Rupp adds:

It was finally decided that when the Indulgence should be promulgated on behalf of rebuilding St. Peter's, Rome, half the proceeds should, by private agreement, go to Albert and the Fuggers. To this indulgence were attached four privileges: "The first, the plenary remission of all sins; the second, a confessional letter allowing the penitent to choose his confessor; the third is the participation in the merits of the saints; the fourth is for the souls in purgatory." Albert's own instructions to his sub-commissary are carefully worded to include the phrase *corde contritus et ore confessus*, i.e. they presuppose contrition and confession.[25]

Albert's instructions were clearly designed to deny that forgiveness of sin was being offered for sale. Rather the payment for indulgences was linked to almsgiving, a traditional work of satisfaction that would meet part, but not all, of the requirements set forth in the sacrament of penance. Contrition and confession were still regarded as necessary conditions of this sacrament.

Also linked to the question of indulgences was the matter of relics. Wittenberg itself was a major relic center due to the zeal of Luther's protector, Duke Frederick, Elector of Saxony. ". . . Saxony had collected almost 18,000 relics, ranging from a twig from Moses' burning bush to a tear that Jesus shed when he wept over Jerusalem. Money from this traffic in relics provided the endowment for the

University of Wittenberg. Pilgrims came from miles around, for by making the proper prayers and offerings, one could earn indulgences which would cancel out 1,902,202 years in purgatory."[26]

Johann Tetzel was not careful when stating the terms of indulgences. He preached to the people with great zeal. He went in procession with the papal bull resting on a satin cushion. The pope's banner was displayed in full pageantry. Tetzel preached such words as these:

> You should know: whoever has confessed and is contrite and puts alms into the box, as his confessor counsels him, will have all of his sins forgiven. . . . So why are you standing about idly? Run, all of you, for the salvation of your souls. . . . Do you not hear the voices of your dead parents and other people, screaming and saying: "Have pity on me, have pity on me. . . . We are suffering severe punishments and pain, from which you could rescue us. . . ."[27]

It was this crass peddling of indulgences that prompted Luther's famous response, the *Ninety-Five Theses.*

Ninety-Five Theses

On October 31, 1517, Martin Luther nailed his famous *Ninety-Five Theses* on the door of the Castle church in Wittenberg. It was Halloween, or more properly speaking, the eve of All Saints' Day. All Saints' Day was a festive occasion drawing hordes of pilgrims to Wittenberg, with its multitudinous relics, to receive indulgences.

Luther's posting of such theses was not a radical act, nor did it desecrate the church's door. Announcements were posted there routinely, making it a sort of community bulletin board. It was customary for the university faculty to hold discussions of theological import, and these discussions were announced in this manner.

Luther penned the theses, not in the German vernacular, but in Latin. This vindicates Luther's later claim that he originally intended to offer the theses for theological discussion, not to create a public uproar.

In the theses Luther addressed what he perceived to be abuses and distortions occurring in connection with the sale of indulgences. Harold Grimm notes: "The Ninety-five Theses show Luther's respect for the sacraments, institutions, and offices of the church. He came to the defense of the pope, whose authority he believed [to be] threatened by the exaggerated pretensions and huckstering attitude of the indulgence preachers. . . ."[28]

Luther especially criticized the crass sales techniques of Johann Tetzel. Thesis 27 said, "They preach human folly who pretend that as soon as money in the coffer rings, a soul from purgatory springs."[29]

Luther's main thrust may have been the abuses and excesses of Tetzel, but in the process Luther raised serious questions about the whole matter of indulgences. He stressed true repentance and asserted that the value of indulgences extends to this world only, not to souls in purgatory.

Luther also raised questions about the treasury of merits and its link to the sacrament of penance. Heiko Oberman observes: ". . . it is already obvious that the ninety-five theses were criticizing more than indulgences. Luther went one bold step further in his thoughts about the Church and the treasures of the Church: 'Every true Christian participates in the treasures of the Church, even without letters of indulgence' (thesis 37); 'this treasure is the Gospel of the glory and grace of God' (thesis 62). In the ensuing controversy over the Gospel of grace, this guiding principle became an actuating force."[30]

One of the great ironies of history is that without a new technology only recently made available, Luther's "protest" may have been a tempest in a small teapot, limited to the faculty at Wittenberg. The recent development of the printing press changed all that. Against Luther's wishes his theses were translated into German, printed en masse, and circulated across the entire German nation within barely two weeks. That fortnight was pivotal for Christian history. Luther later decried this wildfire spread of his theses: "The publicity did not appeal to me. For . . . I myself did not know what an indulgence was, and the song was getting too high for my voice."[31]

It was too late for Luther's voice to crack. Tetzel responded with counter theses stressing the authority of the pope. Among Tetzel's theses were these:

> 5. Christians should be taught that the judgment of the Pope, in those matters that are of faith and necessary to man's salvation, cannot err in the least. . . .
> 22. Christians should be taught that those who cherish deliberate doubts concerning the faith should be most clearly condemned as heretics.
>   . . . For a beast that has touched the mountain shall be stoned.[32]

Tetzel got his wish. Luther sent a copy of his theses to Archbishop Albert of Mainz, for whom Tetzel was working, and asked for a reply. Instead of replying to Luther, Albert forwarded the theses to Rome. Pope Leo initially viewed the matter as an intramural squabble of no great significance, and he refused to intervene.

Tetzel and associates pressed the matter. Aware that John of Wesel had previously been imprisoned for heresy after preaching against indulgences, Tetzel's order sent a formal denunciation of Luther to the curia in January 1518.

Disputation at Augsburg

Luther also incurred the wrath of one of Germany's most articulate and respected theologians, Johann Eck. Eck had earlier met Luther personally, and the two had become friends in 1517. Eck, however, wrote a strong attack against Luther's theses. Eck called Luther a "Bohemian" and linked him with Jan Hus, who had been burned at the stake as a heretic.

In a short time the controversy escalated, leading to a disputation at Augsburg with Cardinal Cajetan, general of the Dominican order. Cajetan was heralded as the most learned theologian of the Roman curia. Luther went to Augsburg certain that it would mean his death if he refused to recant. The meeting was a disaster. Cajetan repeatedly insisted that Luther recant, and Luther

Fig. 3.2
Martin Luther from 1517 to 1521

Luther posts *Ninety-Five Theses*	Oct. 1517
Luther meets Cardinal Cajetan in disputation at Augsburg	Oct. 1518
Luther meets Eck in disputation at Leipzig	July 1519
Luther is condemned by Pope Leo X as heretic	June 1520
Luther is excommunicated by Pope Leo X	Jan. 1521
Luther is condemned at the Diet of Worms	April 1521

refused. He said, "I could not bring myself to say those six letters, REVOCO ['I recant']!"[33]

Luther debated Cajetan on the subject of Pope Clement VI's bull *Unigenitus*. Cajetan maneuvered Luther into raising questions about the pope's authority. The meeting ended abruptly with Luther being whisked away by his friends to escape the wrath of the church, leaving a furious Cajetan to remark that Luther was guilty of damnable errors.

A second crucial disputation took place in July 1519, this time at Leipzig with Johann Eck. This event was attended by Luther and his colleagues Karlstadt and Philipp Melanchthon. Again Eck raised the matter of Luther's link to the heresies of Jan Hus, to which Luther made this sensational reply: among the articles of Jan Hus and the Hussites which were condemned are "many which are truly Christian and evangelical, and which the Church Universal cannot condemn!"[34]

The disputations at Augsburg and Leipzig had left Luther denying first the absolute authority of the pope, and second the authority of church councils. It was in these debates that the Reformation battle cry of *sola Scriptura* was forged.

In the months that followed, Luther published widely and became a hero to the German nation. In the spring of 1520 Pope Leo X appointed a new commission to evaluate Luther's teachings. The commission, which included both Cajetan and Eck, condemned Luther in a bull listing forty-one errors.

The papal bull, *Exsurge Domine,* was signed on June 15, 1520. It received its name from its opening words in Latin, which mean "Arise, O Lord." It declared that a "wild boar is loose" in the vineyard of Christ. The bull condemned Luther as a heretic, and it demanded that he retract his heresies within sixty days or be excommunicated. It exhorted all Christians to reject Luther's heresies and to burn his writings. Luther was not officially excommunicated until the following January, when a supplementary bull was issued.

On December 10, 1520, when the grace period expired, Luther publicly burned a copy of *Exsurge Domine* in a large bonfire. The road to Worms was now paved with stone. The wild boar was loose and nothing would stop him.

The third act [*of saving faith*] *is...
a persuasion of the practical intellect
by which we judge the gospel
to be not only true,
but also good and
therefore most worthy
of our love and desire....*

Francis Turretin

Justification and Faith

fter the Diet of Worms the conflict between Protestants and Rome escalated. The issues at once proliferated far beyond the matter of indulgences, yet they focused chiefly on the substantive issue of justification by faith alone. It has often been noted by the use of an ancient Aristotelian distinction between form and matter that the formal cause of the Reformation was the issue of authority (*sola Scriptura*) and that the material cause was the issue of justification (*sola fide*). (See fig. 1.1.)

Martin Luther came to the conclusion that the central issue was *sola fide*. Hence his well-known assertion that *sola fide* is "the article with and by which the church stands, without which it falls" (*articulus stantis et cadentis ecclesiae*).[1] Luther said of justification: "The article of justification is the master and prince, the lord, the ruler, and the judge over all kinds of doctrines; it preserves and governs all church doctrine and raises up our conscience before God. Without this article the world is utter death and darkness."[2]

Elsewhere Luther wrote: "If the article of justification is lost, all Christian doctrine is lost at the same time."[3]

Luther was not alone in regarding justification by faith alone with such singular importance. John Calvin likewise attached crucial importance to it: "The doctrine of Justification . . . is the principal ground on which religion must be supported, so it requires greater care and attention. For unless you understand first of all what your position is before God, and what the judgment [is] which he passes upon you, you have no foundation on which your salvation can be laid, or on which piety towards God can be reared."[4]

Both Luther and Calvin expressed the singular importance of justification with the metaphor of a *foundation*. Of course both men understood that the biblical metaphor of foundation is that of the prophets and apostles, a foundation that is laid in Christ, the Chief Cornerstone.

But their use of the image of foundation is linked to the central importance of the gospel itself. It is basic or foundational to salvation, inasmuch as it contains the essence of how a person is redeemed. It is not merely the foundation for a building, edifice, or institution; it is foundational to religious life and piety.

The Reformers saw the issue as not only foundational, but also systemic. What began as a dispute over indulgences rapidly spread to a host of other issues, and this indicates the systemic character of the material issue. It is not that Rome and the Reformers had a disagreement over semantics or a technical point of doctrine. The conflict was, and remains, systemic. Disputes over the role of sacraments, Mary, the mass, purgatory, and papal authority may be distinguished from the issue of *sola fide*, but not separated from it. They are intimately related to each other in systemic fashion. At the heart of the systemic conflict is the issue of *sola fide*.

In his introduction to James Buchanan's classic work, *The Doctrine of Justification*, J. I. Packer comments on Luther's formula *articulus stantis et cadentis ecclesiae*:

By this he meant that when this doctrine is understood, believed, and preached, as it was in New Testament times, the church stands in the grace of God and is alive; but where it is neglected, overlaid, or denied, as it was in medieval Catholicism, the church falls from grace and its life drains away, leaving it in a state of darkness and death. The reason why the Reformation happened, and Protestant churches came into being, was that Luther and his fellow Reformers believed that Papal Rome had apostatised from the gospel so completely in this respect that no faithful Christian could with a good conscience continue within her ranks.[5]

Packer rightly observes that the issue of justification became an issue, not merely of error or even of heresy, but of apostasy. Rome considered Luther to be apostate. The Reformers likewise considered Rome to be apostate.

Packer goes on to say:

> For the doctrine of justification by faith is like Atlas: it bears a world on its shoulders, the entire evangelical knowledge of saving grace. ... A right view of these things is not possible without a right understanding of justification; so that, when justification falls, all true knowledge of the grace of God in human life falls with it, and then, as Luther said, the church itself falls. A society like the Church of Rome, which is committed by its official creed to pervert the doctrine of justification, has sentenced itself to a distorted understanding of salvation at every point. Nor can these distortions ever be corrected till the Roman doctrine of justification is put right. And something similar happens when Protestants let the thought of justification drop out of their minds: the true knowledge of salvation drops out with it, and cannot be restored till the truth of justification is back in its proper place. When Atlas falls, everything that rested on his shoulders comes crashing down too.[6]

Ayn Rand once wrote a best-selling novel entitled *Atlas Shrugged.*[7] The image of the mythical hero who bore the world on his back evokes a gasp at the thought that he might shrug. For Atlas to shrug is for Atlas to lose his burden and for the world itself to collapse.

We might dismiss these images in a facile manner, assigning them to the level of hyperbole—intentional exaggerations of the importance of a matter under dispute. Packer and the Reformers could be dismissed as alarmists who overstate the severity of the dispute.

The Importance of Justification

In our day it is evident that though many still affirm *sola fide* in its essential matter, they do not consider its importance to be so great. It may be an important plank in the building, but not in the foundation. It may involve Atlas holding up a straw, but certainly not a world. What Packer declared to be "demonstrably the essence of the biblical message" is in danger of being reduced in importance to the level of a concluding unscientific postscript. (In *ECT sola fide* did not even rate a p.s.)

S*ola fide* is important not merely because the church stands or falls on it. It is important because on it *we* stand or fall. The place where and the time when we will either stand or fall is at the judgment seat of God.

The doctrine of justification has to do with our status before the just judgment of God. That every person will ultimately be called into account before God is central to the teaching of Jesus. He warns that the secret things of our lives will be made manifest before the Father and that every idle word we have spoken will be brought into judgment. The whole world—every man, woman, and child—will come before the final divine tribunal. We will all come to that place, at that time, as either unjustified or justified sinners. Paul at Mars Hill warned: "Truly, these times of ignorance God overlooked, but now commands all men everywhere to repent, 'because He has appointed a day on which He will judge the world in righteousness by the Man whom He has ordained'" (Acts 17:30–31 NKJV).

This judgment will be a righteous judgment by a righteous God. Those who will be judged are unrighteous people. The universality of sin is clearly affirmed by Paul:

> For we have previously charged both Jews and Greeks that they are *all* [italics mine] under sin. As it is written: "There is none righteous, no, not one. . . ." Now we know that whatever the law says,

it says to those who are under the law, that every mouth may be stopped, and all the world may become guilty before God. Therefore by the deeds of the law no flesh will be justified in His sight, for by the law *is* the knowledge of sin. (Rom. 3:9–10, 19–20 NKJV)

Herein is our dilemma. There will be a judgment. It will be a righteous judgment. As fallen, we are not righteous.

The ominous warning of the apostle is that "no flesh will be justified in His sight." Fortunately this is not the whole sentence. It is not an absolute denial of justification. If there will be *no* justification in his sight, then all disputes about the *way* of justification would be vain disputes, much ado about nothing. If there is *no* justification, then there is no gospel—no good news, only bad news.

But this is not the entire statement. Paul does not say there will be no justification. What he does say is that no flesh will be justified in God's sight *by the deeds of the law.*

Paul does not exclude justification altogether. He does exclude it by virtue of our doing deeds of the law. Justification on the ground of our works is eliminated as an option. Christians were once debtors who could not pay their debts to God. The law of God requires perfection. It is a requirement sinners do not and cannot meet. Because of the universal reality of sin, Paul comes to his "therefore." Our sin leads to the necessary inference contained in the conclusion that by the deeds of the law no flesh will be justified in God's sight.

The verdict of the law on sinners was known in the Old Testament. Psalm 130 asks a question that is clearly rhetorical: "If You, LORD, should mark iniquities, O Lord, who could stand?" (130:3 NKJV).

The answer to the psalmist's question is abundantly clear. Who could stand? No one. Certainly not I. Certainly not you. If we are judged by the law in terms of our own righteousness, we will not stand; we are certainly fallen. If Luther rested on his own righteousness before the diet of heaven, he would have to declare: "Here I fall! I can do no other, God help me."

Not only Luther would fall. The whole church—nay, the whole world—would fall.

Paul does not leave us falling without hope before the righteous law of God. He continues his teaching of the doctrine of justification with a single word that screams relief to guilty sinners: "But . . ." There is, to our everlasting benefit, a "however" to his declaration. This little *however* introduces a high and mighty exception to the dreadful conclusion that by the deeds of the law no flesh will be justified in God's sight. Though justification is categorically denied by one means, it is now categorically affirmed by another means. That no flesh will be justified is not the final word. There is another word, which is the gospel itself:

> But now the righteousness of God apart from the law is revealed, being witnessed by the Law and the Prophets, even the righteousness of God *which is* through faith in Jesus Christ to all and on all who believe. For there is no difference; for all have sinned and fall short of the glory of God, being justified freely by His grace through the redemption that is in Christ Jesus, whom God set forth *to be* a propitiation by His blood, through faith, to demonstrate His righteousness, because in His forbearance God had passed over the sins that were previously committed, to demonstrate at the present time His righteousness, that He might be just and the justifier of the one who has faith in Jesus. (Rom. 3:21–26 NKJV)

Here Paul declares a way of justification different from justification by deeds of the law. It is not a novelty, proclaimed for the first time in the New Testament. This way of justification is witnessed to by the Prophets and by the law itself. It is justification through faith in Jesus Christ. This justification is not given to everyone. It is provided *to all*, and *on all*, who believe. It is based on the righteousness of God that is provided *to* and *on* the believer. It is given both freely and graciously by God through the redeeming work of Christ. This manner of justification demonstrates God himself to be both *just* and the *justifier*.

Again, the dilemma faced by the sinner summoned to the judgment seat of God is this: The sinner must appear before a divine Judge who is perfectly just. Yet the sinner is unjust. How can he possibly be unjust and justified? The answer to this question touches the eye of the Reformation tornado. For God to justify the impious (*iustificatio impii*) and himself remain just in the process, the sinner must *somehow* become actually just by a righteousness supplied him by another.

The Ground of Justification

Later we will explore in greater detail the critical difference in how this question is answered by Rome and by the Reformers. Now we merely note in passing that we are either justified by a righteousness that inheres within us or by someone else's righteousness attributed or given to us. Does faith enable us to become actively righteous so that God will declare us righteous? Or does God declare us righteous before we actually become actively righteous by imputing to us the righteousness of Christ?

The conflict over justification by faith alone boils down to this: Is the ground of our justification the righteousness of Christ imputed *to* us, or the righteousness of Christ working *within* us? For the Reformers the doctrine of justification by faith alone meant justification by Christ and his righteousness alone.

Sola fide declares that the ground of our justification is solely the righteousness of Christ. It is a righteousness that is *extra nos*. It is apart from or outside of us, not a part of us, before faith. Luther stated it this way:

> [A Christian] is righteous and holy by an alien or foreign holiness— I call it this for the sake of instruction—that is, he is righteous by the mercy and grace of God. This mercy and grace is not something human; it is not some sort of disposition or quality in the heart. It is a divine blessing, given us through the true knowledge of the Gospel, when we know or believe that our sin has been forgiven through the grace and merit of Christ. . . . Is not this righteousness an alien righteousness? It consists completely in the indulgence of another and is a pure gift of God, who shows mercy and favor for Christ's sake. . . .[8]

The doctrine of *sola fide* speaks of a justification that is *by* faith. The *by* or *through* here in view has to do with the *means* by which justification is appropriated to the believer. At the time of the Reformation the language and philosophical categories of Aristotle were still in vogue. Aristotle had distinguished among various kinds of causes: formal, final, material, efficient, and instrumental.

To gain a picture of Aristotelian categories of causality, let us examine the following analogy. When an artist (sculptor) creates a beautiful work of art (the sculpture), there are various causes at work in the process. The *material cause* of a statue may be the original block of stone out of which the sculpture is fashioned. Here the material cause is the stuff "out of which" a thing is made

Fig. 4.1
Aristotle's Causes

	Definition	Example
Material cause	That out of which something is made.	The stone out of which a statue is carved.
Formal cause	The design or idea followed in the process of making something.	A sketch made by the sculptor as a pattern for the sculpture.
Final cause	The purpose for which something is made.	The reason why the sculptor is doing the sculpture.
Efficient cause	The chief agent causing something to be made.	The sculptor.
Instrumental cause	The means or instrument by which something is made.	The sculptor's chisel.

or shaped. The *formal cause* is the idea, blueprint, or concept the artist uses to "form" his work. The *final cause* is the *purpose* for which the work is crafted (perhaps to beautify one's garden). The *efficient cause* is the agent who makes it all happen. In this case it is the sculptor himself. The *instrumental cause* is the means used to shape the stone. In the case of the statue, the chisel serves as the tool or "instrument" by which the artist shapes the stone.

During the Reformation one point of dispute focused on the *instrumental cause* of justification. Rome declared that there are two instrumental causes of justification: the first is the sacrament of baptism, the second is the sacrament of penance. Therefore Rome could speak of justification *by* the sacraments. By and through the sacraments the grace of justification is received. The sacraments are the *means by which* justifying grace is received.

In the Reformation formula, "Justification is by faith alone," the word *by* captures the idea and communicates the notion that *faith,* not the sacraments, is the instrumental cause of justification. Faith is the instrument by which we are linked to Christ and receive the grace of justification.

A sharp dispute arose over the nature of saving faith. If faith is the all-important instrumental cause and necessary condition for justification, what is essential to it? What are the necessary ingredients of saving faith?

Later we shall explore the difficult question of the harmony between Paul's teaching and James's teaching on the relationship between faith and works. For now it is important to note that, whatever else is involved in saving faith, it is not a "dead faith." Saving faith was declared by Luther to be a *fides viva,* "a vital and living faith."

During the Reformation a threefold definition of saving faith emerged. The constituent elements of saving faith are (1) *notitia,* (2) *assensus,* and (3) *fiducia.* Each element was regarded as necessary for saving faith. None of these elements, even *fiducia,* taken alone or separately, is a *sufficient* condition for saving faith. All three are essential to it.

Faith and Knowledge

The element of *notitia* (or *notae*) refers to knowledge. Though faith is not identical to knowledge, it is not devoid of knowledge. Saving faith does not occur in an intellectual vacuum. It is not ignorance or superstition masquerading as faith. There is a crucial difference between authentic faith and credulity.

Superstition confuses reality and fantasy, truth and falsehood. Superstition is the hallmark of magic and paganism. People indeed "believe in" superstitious things, but such faith has nothing to do with the saving faith of which Scripture speaks. The intrusive power of superstition is great, attested to repeatedly in the Old Testament. Israel displayed a proclivity for syncretism, an irreligious blending or mixing of elements of pagan religion into the content of divinely revealed truth. Nor is the New Testament unaware of the seductive power of sorcery, magic, and superstition that threatened the early church. No period of church history has escaped the influence of spurious faith and superstitious credulity. The modern era is replete with evidence of New Age and occultic ideas embraced by professing Christians.

Notitia has to do with the *content* of faith, the data or information to be received, understood, and embraced. Faith has a clear and rational *object*. What we believe has eternal consequences.

A popular aphorism repeated *ad infinitum* (and indeed *ad nauseam*) in our day is this: "It doesn't matter what you believe as long as you are sincere." This "credo" is on a collision course with Christianity. It preaches another gospel of "justification by faith," which reveals, after a momentary second glance, that it is the very antithesis of the gospel and of *sola fide*. This reduces justification by faith alone to justification by sincerity alone.

The distortion is easy to see. It is a counterfeit concept that rests and depends on a genuine truth for its currency value. The genuine element is the element of sincerity in faith. An insincere faith justifies no one. It is a sham and has no redemptive value. Saving faith must be and is sincere faith. But it is sincere faith in a true object, in true content, not a sincere faith in false content. A person may sincerely believe that Baal is God. His faith is "sincere" insofar as he truly believes that the proposition "Baal is God" is true. Yet my believing that a proposition is true does not make it true.

To say it does not matter what we believe as long as we believe it sincerely is to drive a sword into the heart of Christianity. It is the crassest form of relativism and subjectivism.

We live in an era that boasts of its vehement resistance to propositional truth. Truth is said to be a "relationship" or "personal encounter." Existential philosophy has placed so much stress on the personal and relational character of faith that an allergy has developed against propositional or objective truth.

Again, the distortion of the counterfeit rests on the genuine for its persuasive force. Christian faith certainly does involve and require a personal, relational, subjective response. Faith is not the activity of a disinterested spectator. The passion of personal involvement and commitment of which Søren Kierkegaard wrote is certainly necessary to saving faith. But personal encounter does not negate objective and propositional truth; indeed it presupposes it. I cannot have faith in nothing. My faith must have content or an object. Before I can have a personal relationship with God or anyone else, I must first be aware of them to some degree. I must have some intelligible understanding of what or whom I am believing. I cannot have God in my heart if he is not in my head. Before I can believe *in*, I must believe *that*.

It is possible to be aware of a proposition and even affirm the truth of that proposition and still lack a personal faith in it. But I cannot have the personal relationship *without* any understanding, information, or knowledge of the object of my faith. A faith without an object is sheer subjectivism.

Indeed such subjectivism is not possible. There still remains an object to such faith. It is the subject himself who becomes his own object. A faith relationship by definition requires both a subject and an object. It involves the one who believes (subject) and that which is believed (object).

Notitia then refers to the content of faith. To be saved one must believe certain basic information. It may be a bare minimum, but it is something. For example, to be justified by faith one must believe that there is a God by whom and before whom we are justified. To be saved we may not require an exhaustive or comprehensive knowledge of God, for none of us possesses such comprehensive knowledge, but we must have some knowledge and we must have some *right* knowledge about God. If we believe God is an impersonal, cosmic force, that wrong knowledge about God will not justify us. Indeed it will convict us of idolatry.

If we say we believe in Jesus and mean by this (like some modern theologians) that the name *Jesus* is a "symbol" for the ongoing struggle for human freedom, then the "Jesus" we believe in will not save us because it is no real Jesus at all. Our answer to the question Jesus asked his disciples, "Who do you say that I am?" requires a modicum of correctness for the content of our faith to be saving.

The task of proclaiming the gospel includes more than an imparting of information, but not less. It demands a constant clarification of the content of the gospel. Since its inception the church has struggled against error, distortions, and heresies of all sorts, all of which work against a true understanding of the gospel. Christianity necessarily and intrinsically involves doctrine. Again, it is more than doctrine but by no means less. The right believing of right doctrine is at least to some degree a necessary condition for justification and therefore for salvation. Right doctrine protects the believer from falsehood and superstition.

The power of superstition is enormous and represents a clear and present peril to the soul. Luther said that "superstition is a pernicious emperor who rules in the world throughout the ages and whose rule the people of the world are glad to accept."[9]

Faith and Assent

As the Latin word *assensus* suggests, the second essential element of saving faith is intellectual assent. Intellectual assent involves the assurance or conviction that a certain proposition is true. When we say that we believe George Washington was the first president of the United States, we mean that we affirm the truth of that proposition. This is not faith of a religious sort, but it is integral to a person's belief-system concerning real states of affairs.

At this level, faith is not a matter of volition. We may at times act on the hope that something is true when we are quite uncertain about it. Such action requires a decision. This may be what is meant by a "leap of faith." It is a leap into a certain darkness, which requires a strong element of risk.

However uncertain a proposition may be or however risky is a decision to act upon it, the actual assurance of the truth in question is not determined by the will. I cannot "decide" to be convinced of the truth of a proposition if in fact I am not persuaded of it.

There is great confusion on this point in the religious world. Deciding to believe something is often regarded as a spiritual virtue. In reality it is a perverse attempt at manipulation. Telling a blind person to believe he can see when he cannot see makes as much sense as telling a person to fly when he cannot fly. Saving faith involves assent to what is true, not what is false. There is no virtue in affirming the truth of what is false. Indeed such an affirmation is a vice.

But what if the proposition in question is actually true? Is it not then a virtue to decide to believe it? Take for example the proposition that Jesus' death on the cross was an atonement for sin. Let us assume for the sake of argument that the proposition is not only true but is supported by compelling reasons. It is still possible for a person not to be convinced of it. He may be ignorant of the evidence. He may have been taught by expert skeptics that it is a myth, and his doubt about it may be powerful. That person may "try" to believe it by an act of the will, but such a decision is incapable of yielding faith.

A person may decide to act on the question in various ways. He may resolve to study the matter more closely, to examine the evidence. As a result of this decision to act he may actually come to the place that he gives mental assent to the truth of the proposition. This approaches what St. Augustine described as a *provisional faith*. This faith involves taking provisional steps while still in doubt about the matter in question, steps that may indeed bring clarity and conviction.

There is another side to this coin. We make an important distinction in the arena of apologetics between proof and persuasion. A certain proposition may be proven objectively to be true, and a person may be unpersuaded by the proof. There can be various reasons for this. A person may be so prejudiced or hostile to the proposition that he will not honestly weigh the evidence. Or he may simply be careless or sloppy in his thinking to the degree that he misses the objective cogency of the argument.

On the other hand, a person may be convinced of the truth of a true proposition for poor reasons. He may affirm a true proposition on faulty grounds and "hold" the truth by mere good fortune.

There is still another twist to this point. A person may easily profess to believe something that in fact his mind rejects, or profess to reject a proposition that his mind actually affirms. Just as one cannot create intellectual assent by a volitional decision, so one cannot create non-assent of the mind to a proposition the mind knows is true.

Consider the case of Satan and his demons. The demons were among the first to recognize the true identity of Jesus. They were aware of the proposition "Jesus is the Son of God." They had the *notitia,* and they assented to the truth of the proposition. But they did not have saving faith because they lacked the element of saving *fiducia.*

James got at this when he wrote: "You believe that God is one; you do well, even the demons believe this and tremble" (2:19). Here sarcasm drips from the apostolic pen. James was making the point that meeting the first two necessary conditions of saving faith does not guarantee salvation. It merely qualifies one to be a demon. If the third necessary condition is absent, then the other two are insufficient for justification. Again, these conditions considered separately are necessary but not sufficient conditions.

Intellectual assent or personal assurance of the truth of propositions admits to degrees. Though not a matter of mere subjectivism, it does involve the subjective state of the believer's mind. Insofar as assurance is a matter of degrees, it admits to augmentation or diminution. That is, we can be "more or less" certain of the truth of a given proposition.

Herman Witsius, the seventeenth-century Dutch theologian, writes:

Plērophoria, "full assurance," is an expression which occurs more than once in the writings of the Apostle Paul. He speaks of *plērophoria suneseōs,* "the full assurance of understanding" (Col. 2:2); *plērophoria tēs elpidos,* "the full assurance of hope" (Heb. 6:11); and *plērophoria pisteōs,* "the full assurance of faith" (Heb. 10:22). According to its etymology, this word denotes "a carrying with full sail"; the metaphor being taken, probably, from ships when their sails are filled with favourable gales. Thus it may here signify the vehement inclination of the mind, impelled by the Holy Spirit, towards an assent to the truth perceived.[10]

Francis Turretin adds: "As indeed philosophers observe three degrees of perfection in assent (to wit, firmness, certainty and evidence); firmness that it may be without hesitation; certainty that it may rest upon a certain and solid foundation; evidence that it may not rest upon another's testimony, but be proved either by the senses or by reason (as in science)."[11]

Luther spoke of the importance of assurance in true faith, though he also acknowledged the difference between strong and weak faith. He said:

> Faith is and, indeed, must be a steadfastness (*ein Standfest*) of the heart, which does not waver, wobble, shake, tremble, or doubt, but stands firm and is sure of its case. . . . When this Word enters the heart by true faith, it makes the heart as firm, sure, and certain as it is itself, so that the heart is unmoved, stubborn, and hard in the face of every temptation, the devil, death, and anything whatever, boldly and proudly despising and mocking everything that spells doubt, fear, evil, and wrath. For it knows that God's Word cannot lie.[12]

Luther distinguished both between a weak and a strong faith and between a weak and a *wrong* faith. On the former distinction he declared:

> It is, of course, true that I and you do not hold and believe the saving truth so firmly as St. Peter does. Yet we have one and the same treasure. Two persons may hold glasses of wine in their hands: the hand of the one trembles, the hand of the other does not. Two

persons may hold a purse full of money: one with a weak hand, the other with a strong hand. Whether the hand is strong or weak, please God, it neither increases nor decreases the contents of the purse. So the only difference between me and St. Peter is the fact that he holds this treasure more firmly.[13]

With respect to the distinction between a weak faith and a wrong faith, Luther declared:

Indeed, all three truths must be believed: that Christ is God, that He is man, and that He became man for us, as the Apostles' Creed teaches: conceived by the Holy Spirit. . . . If one item of this creed is lacking, all items must fall. Faith must be complete and embrace everything. Although it may be weak and subject to trial, it must in any case be complete (*ganz*) and not false. To be weak in the faith does not do the damage, but to be wrong—that is eternal death.[14]

The first two elements of saving faith, *notitia* and *assensus,* are matters of the mind. That is, they are cognitive, involving awareness of information and intellectual assent to the truth of that information. The lack of *notitia* involves ignorance or improper understanding. The lack of *assensus* involves the lack of loving affirmation of truth. Saving faith requires at least rudimentary awareness of essential truth and the persuasion that it is indeed truth.

Faith and *Fiducia*

The third element of saving faith, *fiducia,* involves a "plus" to the cognitive element (although Gordon Clark makes a fascinating case that even this added element is at root intellectual). Leaving Clark aside for the moment, we observe that in historic Reformational expressions of the distinctive elements of faith, a sharp distinction is made between the cognitive dimensions of faith and the affective and volitional dimensions. Here we find numerous references to the "heart" or to the disposition of the soul.

The language of Scripture regarding constituent parts of a human being, especially with respect to thought and action, is complex and at times difficult to unravel. The classical and ongoing contemporary debate between trichotomism and dichotomy attest to this. The Bible does not speak in the language of *Gray's Anatomy*. At times the word *heart* is used interchangeably with the word *mind* or *spirit* or even *soul*. At other times these are used in figurative or metaphorical ways, sometimes being distinguished and at other times being virtually identified with each other.

The Old Testament declares: "As a man thinks in his heart, so is he" (Prov. 23:7). This verse is clearly not intended to suggest that the primary organ of thought is a muscle in the chest that pumps blood. The writer understood (at least to some degree) the biological difference between the brain and the heart. When he speaks of the "heart" thinking, he is speaking of the thinking that reaches the depth or "core" of our being. This thinking penetrates the surface of mere awareness or reflection and takes anchor in the soul. This could simply refer to the various levels of intensity with which a truth is known or affirmed. It is what some refer to as "core beliefs."

When considering the impact that ideas, propositions, and thoughts have on our lives, we may distinguish among various levels or stages of intensity. Consider the commandment "Thou shalt not steal" as an example. Before I can act with any virtue of obedience or vice of disobedience with respect to this law, I must first be *conscious* or aware of it. The Bible declares that where there is no knowledge of the law there is no transgression. (This has technical ramifications where distinctions are necessary for the sake of precision, but we are interested here simply in the broad concern.)

Our response to such a law, our behavior with respect to it, is related to our degree of *consciousness, conviction*, and *conscience*. For a truth to take root in our conscience, we must first be conscious of it. We can be aware that God says we must not steal but have no conviction about the matter. One role of the Holy Spirit is to convict us of sin and of righteousness. We must be not only aware or conscious of the law, but also convinced of its import before it becomes a matter of conscience. Yet it remains possible for a person to be aware or conscious that stealing is wrong and continue to steal. A person may be convinced that it is wrong and continue to steal. Once it becomes a matter of conscience, it is still possible to commit the sin. We are capable and indeed often proficient in acting against our consciences. Luther was right when he declared at Worms that it is "neither right nor safe" to act against conscience.

The conscience, as St. Thomas Aquinas maintained, can act as both *accuser* and *excuser.* It plays both roles. When a law becomes a matter of conscience with us, this does not guarantee we will obey it. We all know the experience of doing something we are conscious is wrong, convinced is wrong, and of having our consciences howl in protest.

Conscience does not abolish sin, but it does retard it. Its power of retardation is linked to the degree of intensity with which the conscience is endowed. The strengthening of conscience is vital to our sanctification. That it can be strong or weak, however, attests to the matter with which we are presently concerned: the depth dimension of faith.

The element of *fiducia* probes the depth dimension that involves not only the cognitive but the affective and volitional response. When Gordon Clark objects to separating these elements from each other, he is correct. They must not be separated even though we may be inclined to do so. In Jonathan Edwards's epic work *The Freedom of the Will,*[15] he defines the will as "the mind choosing." Here the act of choosing (which may be distinguished actively from the act of thinking and can therefore be attributed to something we call "will") is not the action of some organ that exists independent of the mind. If an action is indeed voluntary, if it involves a conscious choice, it is clearly an activity of the mind in the first instance.

We frequently distinguish between *thinking* and *desiring.* We use the language of affection with respect to our desires. We speak of strong *feelings* about a goal or aim that we *desire.* We do have such feelings, but these feelings are associated with ideas. To have desire there must be something to desire. We must have an *idea* of the thing we desire. We cannot have an affection for nothing or a desire for something about which we have no idea.

Fiducia means a positive disposition of the soul or mind to an object. To see how this works with respect to the necessary condition for saving faith, let us consider the case of Satan and his response to Christ. Satan does not lack intelligence. He is aware—clearly aware—of the identity of Christ. Satan has the *notitia*. He is also fully cognizant of the *truth* of the identity of Christ. Satan has the *assensus*.

But Satan personally places no *fiducia* or trust in Christ. He resists Christ. He does *will* to oppose Christ. He has no affection for Christ. In fact he despises Christ. His unmitigated hatred for Christ displays itself in an enmity that knows no bounds. The disposition or inclination of Satan's "heart" is utterly negative. Therefore it can be said Satan does not possess "faith" in Christ.

Satan's problem is one of internal corruption—a core corruption, a corruption of the heart. But herein is the sticky point Gordon Clark raises: however much Satan's emotions may color his response to Christ, it is ultimately still a matter of mind and knowledge.

Fundamentally Satan's problem is intellectual. He lacks understanding of the sweetness and excellence of Christ. Satan has no affection for Christ because he sees nothing lovable about Christ. Christ represents an obstacle to Satan for the evil things Satan loves. He knows that Jesus is good. This is why Satan hates him. Satan loves what is evil and detests what is good. He recognizes goodness. But being evil himself and loving evil, he does not love the goodness of goodness.

I do not mean to play word games here. Saving *fiducia* rests on an awakening to the sweetness and loveliness of Christ, an awakening wrought in the minds and souls of corrupt humans by the regenerating power of the Holy Spirit. As Jesus declared to Nicodemus, a person cannot even see the kingdom of God, let alone enter it, unless he is first reborn by the Holy Spirit. The flesh and the mind of flesh are at enmity with God. This reaches its nadir in the "flesh" of Satan.

On the one hand Scripture describes Satan in terms of a kind of advanced intelligence manifested in his guile, craftiness, and cleverness. On the other hand it may be said that Satan is incredibly stupid. He just does not get it. He fails to see the *value* of the *truth* or the "goodness of goodness."

Value and goodness are not synonyms. Value has to do with the *perceived* worth of something. This is the primary premise of the subjective theory of value in the science of economics. The marketplace works because one person values a thing more highly than another. In the old barter system a shoemaker traded shoes for shirts from the shirtmaker. The shoemaker had more shoes than he needed but no shirts, so he valued a shirt more than a pair of shoes. Likewise the shirtmaker had more shirts than he needed but no shoes, so he was eager to trade shirts for shoes. In the barter exchange both sides profited because both got what they valued more in the circumstances. The modern market still works fundamentally in the same way. Even with currency as the medium of exchange, we are involved simply in a more complex and sophisticated form of barter.

Values and ethics get confused when we begin to value things that are bad. Jesus addressed this problem when he raised the rhetorical question, "What will it profit a man if he gains the whole world, and loses his own soul?" (Mark 8:36 NKJV).

Here Jesus makes a statement about the value of a particular act of barter. The man exchanges his soul for the world. He values the world more than he values his soul. In terms of his *perception* of value, he has made a great deal. In terms of Jesus' perception of value, he has made a terrible deal. Indeed he has made a trade that is both evil (because he violates the law of God) and stupid (because in the long run he loses).

When Satan rejects Christ, he does so based on his own value system. He loves evil and hates good. He loves darkness and hates light. He chooses what he values and rejects what he does not value. He has a serious problem with his *perceived values.*

Fallen man is in the same corrupt state. We are by nature children of Satan, imitating and replicating his value system. It is said of man that he, like Satan, loves the darkness rather than the light. What is the reason for our antipathy to the light? Our deeds are evil.

The element of *fiducia* includes a dramatic change in our values. It involves a radical shift in *perceived value*. Insofar as it is a change in *perception*, it is a change in intellectual perception. It is not by accident that the biblical concept of repentance is expressed by the word *metanoieō*, which literally means a "changing of the mind."

For saving faith to occur there must be a real change in the person. The change is rooted in a transformation of one's perception of Christ. The Spirit quickens us and reveals to us something we did not formerly experience, namely the sweetness and excellence of Christ. It is a radical change of perceived value. Where formerly we were hostile or indifferent (a thinly veiled form of hostility) toward Christ, now we perceive him as the Pearl of Great Price that we must possess at all cost.

This certainly involves a change in emotion, disposition, inclination, and volition. We now choose Christ. We embrace Christ. We gladly receive Christ. Indeed we flee to Christ. Reformation theology insists that regeneration that changes the heart of the sinner must *precede* faith. My perception of the value of Christ must change before I will ever embrace him or personally trust him. Without that regenerating change, my response to Christ will mimic Satan's.

Francis Turretin defines *fiducia* as follows: "The third act is fiducial and practical assent or a persuasion of the practical intellect by which we judge the gospel to be not only true, but also good and therefore most worthy of our love and desire; also the promises of grace to be most certain concerning the remission of sins and the bestowal of salvation upon all believers and penitents and so also upon me if I shall believe and repent."[16]

Turretin explores the volitional dimension of *fiducia* when he adds: "Now this persuasion ought not to be only inchoate and half full (which sometimes exists in the reprobate also who receive the word with joy), but full and absolute, determining and drawing after it the will and beholding the gospel object and the promise of grace, not only as true and imbued with a certain good, but also as the highest good proposed to us in God and affording the sole and most sufficient means of salvation in Christ."[17]

The three elements of saving faith—*notitia, assensus,* and *fiducia*—separately and individually lack the force of a sufficient condition. When added together they compose the essence of saving faith and then achieve the level of sufficiency. When these three necessary conditions of saving faith are met, then the faith that is present is a sufficient condition for justification.

We recall that the formula "justification is by faith alone" means that faith (as defined above) is the *instrumental cause* of our justification. This instrumental cause is sufficient for justification and in effect works *ex opere operato.*

Other Aspects of Faith

The threefold delineation of the constituent elements of faith was further refined by later theologians. Both Francis Turretin and Herman Witsius, for example, enlarged on these elements. Turretin lists seven aspects of the act of faith, the three we have examined plus four more.

Act of refuge. This response involves an act of desire by which the believer endeavors to possess Christ. Witsius described this dimension as a hunger and thirst after Christ. He writes: ". . . how is it possible . . . that such a person should not seriously and ardently desire to have Christ dwelling in him, that he should not seek and pant after him, and have so vehement a longing as can be satisfied with nothing short of the possession of the object desired; as hunger and thirst are allayed only by meat and drink?"[18]

Act of reception and union. Of this aspect Turretin declares that it is the act "by which we not only seek Christ through a desire of the soul and fly to him, but apprehend and receive him offered, embrace him found, apply him to ourselves and adhere to and unite ourselves to him."[19] Witsius calls this the *formal and principal* act of faith. By this act of faith the believer becomes united with Christ. This act is what the New Testament speaks of as "receiving" Christ. Witsius says: "By this act, Christ becomes, so to speak, the peculiar property of the believing soul. All that

Fig. 4.2
Francis Turretin's Seven Acts of Faith

1	Act of knowledge (*Notitia*)	Knowing all things to be believed by us, whether pertaining to our misery or to the grace of God.
2	Theoretical assent (*Assensus*)	Receiving as true and divine what we know.
3	Fiducial and practical assent (*Fiducia*)	Judging the gospel to be good and worthy of our love and desire. Judging the promises of grace to be most certain concerning the remission of sins and the bestowal of salvation on all who believe and repent, including myself if I believe and repent.
4	Act of refuge	Betaking ourselves by an act of desire to Christ, seeking in him pardon of sin and salvation.
5	Act of reception and union	Apprehending and receiving Christ, embracing him, applying him to ourselves, adhering to him, and uniting ourselves to him.
6	Reflex act	Concluding that I have believed and therefore that Christ has certainly died for me, I belong to him, and I will assuredly be made happy in him.
7	Act of confidence and consolation	Experiencing the joy, tranquility, peace, acquiescence, and delight that arise from the possession of Christ.

From Francis Turretin, *Institutes of Elenctic Theology,* vol. 2, trans. George Musgrave Giger, ed. James T. Dennison Jr. (Phillipsburg, N.J.: P & R, 1994), pp. 561–63.

belongs to Christ being exhibited together with him, the believer claims to himself whatever is Christ's, and especially his righteousness, which is the foundation of salvation."[20]

Reflex act. In this aspect of faith, the outward direction of faith toward its object (Christ) is reflected back toward the believing subject. Turretin describes this act as that "by which the soul which has thus received Christ (turning itself back upon itself and seeing in its heart the direct act of persuasion, refuge and reception) concludes that it believes and, because it believes, that Christ certainly died for him and belongs to him with all his blessings and that he will assuredly be made happy by him."[21] For Witsius the *reflex act* follows the acts of *resting on Christ* and *surrendering* to him. Witsius says of surrender: ". . . when the believer thus receives Christ and rests upon him, he considers him not merely as a SAVIOUR, but also as a LORD. He receives a whole Christ, and acquiesces in him in all those characters which he sustains: but he is not less a Lord than a Saviour; nay, he cannot be a Saviour, unless he be also a Lord."[22] What Witsius divides into distinctive aspects, Turretin joins together.

Act of confidence and consolation. For Turretin this act consists in "that joy, tranquility, peace, acquiescence and delight which arise from the possession of Christ, by which the believing soul leaning upon its beloved . . . and conscious of its own most intimate union with Christ through faith and sure of its own mutual communion and love with him, piously exults and rejoices in the Lord, glories in adversity and courageously challenges and despises all enemies whatever (Rom. 8:38–39). . . ."[23] Turretin acknowledges that this act is not part of the essence of faith as such, but flows out of faith as a necessary consequence.

These further elaborations of aspects of faith, whose number varies among Reformed theologians like Turretin and Witsius, may also be subsumed under the heading of *fiducia.*

What emerges clearly from this analysis is that the Reformers understood saving faith to be a profound matter. Justifying faith is by no means an empty or merely formal concept. It is a living response to Christ and energetically involves both mind and soul. It is both cognitive and affective. It is not merely speculative, temporary, or presumptuous.

There is no "easy-believism" in the Reformation doctrine of *sola fide.* Saving faith is not vacuous. It is a deep and profound reality. The confidence it yields is not arrogance, but the sweet consolation of assurance that gives rest to the soul.

Witsius differentiates authentic faith from a false and presumptuous faith:

Sometimes they lay as a foundation for their confidence, either a preposterous notion respecting the general mercy of God, and some easy method of salvation which they discover in the Gospel-covenant; or an opinion of the sufficiency of their own holiness, because they are not so extremely vicious as the most daring profligates; or their external communion with the Church and attendance on the public worship; or the security of their sleeping conscience, and the soothing fancies of their own dreams, which they regard as the peace of God, and the consolations of the Holy Spirit.[24]

Saving faith must not be confused with "cheap grace": full assurance cannot rest on church membership or attendance, an exaggerated evaluation of one's own righteousness, or a seared conscience. These are not true marks of grace. By contrast Witsius declares: "But true believers, impressed with a deep sense of their own wretchedness, panting after the grace of the Lord Jesus, and laying hold upon it with a trembling humility, dare not, however, boast of it as already their own, till after diligent investigation they have discovered certain and infallible evidences of grace in themselves."[25]

It is entirely by the intervention of Christ's righteousness that we obtain justification before God.
This is equivalent to saying that man is not just in himself, but that the righteousness of Christ is communicated to him by imputation, while he is strictly deserving of punishment.

John Calvin

Imputed Righteousness:
The Evangelical Doctrine

At the heart of the controversy between Roman Catholic and Reformation theology is the nature of justification itself. It is a debate not merely about how or when or by what means a person is justified, but about the very meaning of justification itself.

Reformed theology insists that the biblical doctrine of justification is *forensic* in nature. What does this mean? In the popular jargon of religion, the word *forensic* is used infrequently. The word is not foreign, however, to ordinary language. It appears daily in the news media, particularly with reference to criminal investigations and trials. We hear of "forensic evidence" and "forensic medicine" as we listen to the reports of criminologists, coroners, and pathologists. Here the term *forensic* refers to the judicial system and judicial proceedings.

The term *forensic* is also used to describe events connected with public speaking. Schools hold forensic contests or events that feature formal debates or the delivery of speeches.

The link between these ordinary usages of *forensic* and its theological use is that justification has to do with a *legal* or *judicial* matter involving some type of declaration. We can reduce its meaning to the concept of *legal declaration.*

The doctrine of justification involves a legal matter of the highest order. Indeed it is the legal issue on which the sinner stands or falls: his status before the supreme tribunal of God.

When we are summoned to appear before the bar of God's judgment, we face a judgment based on perfect justice. The presiding Judge is himself perfectly just. He is also omniscient, fully aware of our every deed, thought, inclination, and word. Measured by the standard of his canon of righteousness, we face the psalmist's rhetorical question that hints at despair: "If you, LORD, should mark iniquities, . . . who could stand?" (Ps. 130:3 NKJV).

The obvious answer to this query is supplied by the Apostle Paul: "There is none righteous, no, not one. . . ." (Rom. 3:10).

God commands us to be holy. Our moral obligation *coram Deo* (before the face of God) is to live perfect lives. One sin mars that obligation and leaves us naked, exposed before divine justice. Once a person sins at all, a perfect record is impossible. Even if we could live perfectly *after* that one sin, we would still fail to achieve perfection. Our sin may be *forgiven,* but forgiveness does not *undo* the sin. The consequences of the sin may be removed or ameliorated, but the sin itself is not undone.

The Bible speaks figuratively about the sin being washed, cleansed, healed, and blotted out. The sin, which is scarlet, may become white as snow, the crimson may become like wool, in God's sight. The sin may be cast into the sea of forgetfulness or purged with hyssop. But these images describe an expiation for sin and divine forgiveness or remission of our sin. Our record does not change, but our guilt does. Hence Paul declares, "Blessed is the man to whom the LORD shall not impute sin" (Rom. 4:8 NKJV).

In our redemptive forgiveness God does not charge us with what we owe. He does not *count* our sins against us. If he did, no one (except Jesus) would ever escape his just wrath. No one but Christ would be able to *stand* before God's judgment.

Again, God in his grace may regenerate us, sanctify us, and even glorify us. He might make us perfect in the future. He really does change the elect and will eventually make the justified totally and completely righteous. But even the perfected saint in heaven was once a sinner and has a track record that, apart from the grace of justification, would send him to hell.

Thus, where temporal creatures are concerned, everyone who is once imperfect is *always* imperfect with respect to the whole scope of the person's individual history. This is what Thomas Aquinas meant when he asserted that justification is always of the impious (*iustificatio impii*). Righteous people have no need of justification, even as the healthy have no need of a physician.

Both Roman Catholic and Reformation theology are concerned with the justification of *sinners.* Both sides recognize that the great human dilemma is how unjust sinners can ever hope to survive a judgment before the court of an absolutely holy and absolutely just God.

If we define *forensic justification* as a legal declaration by which God declares a person just and we leave it at that, we would have no dispute between Rome and Evangelicalism. Though Rome has an antipathy to the concept of forensic justification, this antipathy is directed against the Protestant view of it. In chapter 7 of the sixth session of the Council of Trent, Rome declared: ". . . not only are we reputed but we are truly called and are just, receiving justice within us, each one according to his own measure. . . ."[1]

Here Rome is jealous to distinguish between being *reputed* just and actually *being* just, yet it is still true that God *calls* the baptismally regenerated just. That is, for Rome justification is forensic in that justification involves God's *legal declaration.* A person is justified when God declares that person just. The reason or the ground of that declaration differs radically between Roman Catholic and Reformed theology. But both agree that a legal declaration by God is made.

Nor is it sufficient merely to say that Rome teaches that justification means "to make just," while Protestants teach that justification means "to declare just." For Rome God both makes just and declares just. For Protestants God both makes just and declares just—*but not in the same way.* For Rome the declaration of justice *follows* the making inwardly just of the regenerate sinner. For the Reformation the declaration of justice follows the imputation of Christ's righteousness to the regenerated sinner.

It has been said in this regard that Rome believes justification follows and is based on sanctification, while Evangelicalism believes sanctification follows and is based on justification. This facile distinction has prompted some analysts to suggest that the whole debate is only a matter of semantics and misunderstanding, that both sides believe the same thing. The only difference, these analysts argue, is that what Rome calls justification, Evangelicalism calls sanctification.

The Point at Issue

This misses the entire point of the debate. The real issue is the *ground* of justification and the manner in which justification is effected.

This is not to say that the issue is free of semantic difficulties. A real semantic question has been exaggerated by fluid changes in the language. Alister McGrath notes this problem when he applies semantic-field theory to the concept of justification:

> The *semantic field* of a word includes not merely its synonyms, but also its antonyms, homonyms and homophones. As such, it is much broader than the *lexical field*, which may be defined very precisely in terms of words which are closely associated with one another. . . . The translation of a word into a different language inevitably involves a distortion of the semantic field, so that certain nuances and associations present in the original cannot be conveyed in a translation, and new nuances and associations not already present make their appearance.[2]

The problem McGrath addresses is well known to anyone who has ever been involved in translating documents. McGrath also notes a difference between the *concept* of justification and the *doctrine* of justification: "The *concept* of justification is one of many employed within the Old and New Testaments, particularly the Pauline corpus, to describe God's saving action towards his people. . . . The *doctrine* of justification has come to develop a meaning quite independent of its biblical origins, and concerns the *means by which man's relationship to God is established.*"[3]

We quite agree that the concept of justification differs from the doctrine of justification. It is important to note, however, that this is true within the Scriptures themselves. The biblical doctrine of justification may be *distinguished* from biblical concepts of justification but may not be *separated* from them. The biblical doctrine of justification is made up of the biblical "concepts" regarding justification and merely refers to a precise definition of what is common to their various modes of expression.

Where semantic-field theory comes into play is in the translation of biblical terms into other languages. The problem involves first the translation of the Hebrew *sedaqa* into the Greek *dikaiosynē*, and then into the Latin used by the church fathers and later the Scholastics. The English word *justify* derives from the Latin *iustificare.*

McGrath sees Augustine's treatment of justification as pivotal to the subsequent development of the doctrine of justification in the Roman Catholic Church: "Augustine understands the verb *iustificare* to mean 'to make righteous,' an understanding of the term which he appears to have held throughout his working life. In arriving at this understanding, he appears to have interpreted *-ficare* as the unstressed form of *facere*, by analogy with *vivificare* and *mortificare*. Although this is a permissible interpretation of the *Latin word*, it is unacceptable as an interpretation of the *Hebrew concept* which underlies it."[4]

McGrath goes on to say: "Man's righteousness, effected in justification, is regarded by Augustine as *inherent* rather than *imputed*. . . . The righteousness which man thus receives, although originating from God, is nevertheless located within man, and can be said to be *his*, part of his being and intrinsic to his person."[5]

The question of *inherent* versus *imputed* righteousness goes to the heart of the Reformation debate. When the Reformers spoke of forensic justification, they meant a legal declaration made by God that was based on the *imputation* of Christ's righteousness to the believer, not on Christ's righteousness inherent *in* the believer.

James Buchanan stated as his first proposition of justification that "justification is a legal, or forensic, term, and is used in Scripture to denote the acceptance of any one as righteous in the sight of God."[6]

In a way Buchanan, writing in the nineteenth century, anticipated McGrath's twentieth-century concern about semantic-field theory:

> ... the right interpretation of many passages of Scripture can only be satisfactorily established by a careful inductive inquiry into the *usus loquendi* of the sacred writers. . . . The Scriptural meaning of these terms is to be determined, neither by their mere etymology, nor by the sense which they bear in classical literature, but by the usage of the Hebrew and Greek Scriptures. . . . So far as etymology is concerned, the verb '*to justify*' might possibly mean 'to make righteous inherently'; . . . wherever it is used with reference to our acceptance with God, it can only be understood in a judicial or forensic sense.[7]

Likewise Francis Turretin argued that in the Scriptures *justification* "is never taken for an infusion of righteousness, but as often as the Scriptures speak professedly about our justification, it always must be explained as a forensic term."[8]

Calvin on Justification

Turretin followed John Calvin's view of forensic justification. Like Martin Luther, Calvin insisted that justification is crucial to Christian faith. He writes: "The doctrine of Justification is now to be fully discussed, and discussed under the conviction, that as it is the principal ground on which religion must be supported, so it requires greater care and attention. For unless you understand first of all what your position is before God, and what the judgment [is] which he passes upon you, you have no foundation on which your salvation can be laid, or on which piety towards God can be reared."[9]

Calvin's full exposition of the doctrine of justification demonstrates that at every point he works "under the conviction" that "it is the principal ground on which religion must be supported." This work "under the conviction" is a work that stresses the foundational structure of forensic justification.

At the outset of his exposition, at the point he calls the "very threshold," Calvin writes: "A man is said to be justified in the sight of God when in the judgment of God he is deemed righteous, and is accepted on account of his righteousness; for as iniquity is abominable to God, so neither can the sinner find grace in his sight, so far as he is and so long as he is regarded as a sinner."[10] The key words in this expression are *deemed* and *regarded.* Calvin's point is simple: God will only declare just those whom he regards as just.

But the question remains, How can God ever deem a sinner just? Calvin identifies only two possible ways God can do this: that person is justified either by his own works or by Christ's works. To be justified by works requires that "there can be found a purity and holiness which merits an attestation of righteousness at the throne of God, or if by the perfection of his works he can answer and satisfy the divine justice."[11]

For Calvin, God can declare a person just only if that person *possesses* righteousness. The question is, How does the person possess it? Does he possess it *inherently* or by *imputation*? This is *the* question of the Reformation.

Calvin says of justification by faith:

> . . . a man will be *justified by faith* when, excluded from the righteousness of works, he by faith lays hold of the righteousness of Christ, and clothed in it appears in the sight of God not as a sinner, but as righteous. Thus we simply interpret justification, as the acceptance with which God receives us into his favour as if we were righteous; and we say that this justification consists in the forgiveness of sins and the imputation of the righteousness of Christ.[12]

Calvin uses the biblical metaphor of clothing to describe imputation. In the biblical image the sinner is described either as "naked and ashamed" or as clothed in "filthy rags." The first conscious awareness of sin in Adam and Eve was a sense of being naked. They hid themselves because of their shame. It may be said that the first act of God's redemptive grace occurred when he condescended to clothe his embarrassed fallen creatures.

The image of "covering" occurs frequently in Scripture, particularly in connection with atonement. The accusation of Satan against the priest of Zechariah was directed against the priest's soiled garments. God rebuked Satan and clothed the priest in a way that made him acceptable in God's sight (Zech. 3:1–5). The New Testament speaks of "putting on Christ" (Rom. 13:14) and of Christ being our righteousness.

By imparting or imputing Christ's righteousness to us sinners, God reckons us as just. It is "as if" we were inherently just. But we are not inherently just. We are "counted" or "reckoned" just by imputation.

This is the point of Luther's statement that we are "at the same time just and sinner" *(simul iustus et peccator)*. We are just by imputation even while sin still remains in us, though it does not reign in us.

Calvin goes on to say: "*To justify*, therefore, is nothing else than to acquit from the charge of guilt, as if innocence were proved. Hence, when God justifies us through the intercession of Christ, he does not acquit us on a proof of our own innocence, but by an imputation of righteousness, so that though not righteous in ourselves, we are deemed righteous in Christ."[13]

Calvin cites as an example of justification by faith the case of the publican who went to his house "justified" (Luke 18:14): ". . . it cannot be held that he obtained this justification by any merit of works. All that is said is, that after obtaining the pardon of sins he was regarded in the sight of God as righteous. He was justified, therefore, not by any approval of works, but by gratuitous acquittal on the part of God."[14]

This acquittal rests on the imputation of the righteousness of Christ. Again, when we review Luther's maxim *simul iustus et pec-*

cator, we see imputation as the basis of God's forensic declaration.

By this formula Luther did not mean that the sinner who is still a sinner is therefore an unchanged person. The sinner who has saving faith is a regenerate person. Regeneration effects real change in the person, but the change wrought by regeneration does not effect immediate perfection.

The regenerate person is now indwelled by the Holy Spirit. Nevertheless he remains imperfectly just in himself. The regenerate person is also in a real process of sanctification by which he is *becoming* just. But he by no means reaches that point of perfect justness before God declares him perfectly just in Christ.

Those who possess saving faith necessarily, inevitably, and immediately *begin* to manifest the fruits of faith, which are works of obedience. The ground of the person's justification, however, remains solely and exclusively the imputed righteousness of Christ. It is by his righteousness and his righteousness alone that the sinner is declared to be just and is really just in him.

Christ's Perfect Obedience

Francis Turretin states it this way:

The gospel teaches that what could not be found in us and was to be sought in another, could be found nowhere else than in Christ, the God-man (*theanthrōpō*); who taking upon himself the office of surety most fully satisfied the justice of God by his perfect obedience and thus brought to us an everlasting righteousness by which alone we can be justified before God; in order that covered and clothed with that garment as though it were of our first-born (like Jacob), we may obtain under it the eternal blessing of our heavenly Father.[15]

Turretin makes a crucial point that is often overlooked in popular forms of Evangelicalism today. He speaks of Christ's fully satisfying the justice of God by his perfect obedience. Too often Christ's work of satisfying the justice of God is reduced to his work of atonement. The satisfaction view of the atonement was held by the Reformers. But this work of satisfaction is only one aspect of the matter. We may distinguish between the *negative* and the *positive* aspects of Christ's work of satisfaction. In the atonement Christ satisfies the negative side of God's justice. Here, again by imputation, Christ pays the penalty due our sins. He receives, for us, the punitive wrath of God that our sin deserves. He takes the consequences of our demerits, our unjustness. He receives the judgment due our guilt. In this regard God's justice is satisfied.

The atonement is vicarious because it is accomplished via imputation. Christ is the sin-bearer for his people, the *Agnus Dei* (Lamb of God) who takes away (expiates) our sin and satisfies (propitiates) the demands of God's justice. The cross displays both God's justice (in that he truly punishes sin) and his grace (because he punishes sin by providing a substitute for us).

The atonement also involves a forensic matter. God declares Christ to be "guilty" of sin after the Son willingly bears for his people sins that are imputed or transferred to him. Here is imputation with a vengeance—indeed a divine vengeance. This forensic act of imputed punishment is the very heart of the New Testament message. With no pun intended it is the *crux* of the matter.

The cross alone, however, does not justify us. We need not only a substitute to pay for our demerits, but also positive righteousness. We are justified not only by the *death* of Christ but also by the *life* of Christ.

Christ's mission of redemption was not limited to the cross. To save us he had to live a life of perfect righteousness. His perfect, active obedience was necessary for his and our salvation. He earned the merit of perfect righteousness, not only for his own humanity, but for all those whom he redeems. Christ perfectly fulfilled all demands of the law, meriting by his active obedience the blessing promised in the old covenant.

We are constituted as righteous by the obedience of Christ, which is imputed to us by faith. The New Testament draws a parallel between Adam and Christ, the "new" or "second" Adam. Turretin comments: "'As by the offense of one [supply "guilt"] came upon all men to condemnation, even so by the righteousness of one [*di' henos dikaiōmatos*; supply "the blessing redounded"] upon all men unto justification of life. . . .' The act of one cannot be made the act of many, except by imputation."[16]

Calvin concludes with respect to imputation:

> . . . it is entirely by the intervention of Christ's righteousness that we obtain justification before God. This is equivalent to saying that man is not just in himself, but that the righteousness of Christ is communicated to him by imputation, while he is strictly deserving of punishment. Thus vanishes the absurd dogma, that man is justified by faith, inasmuch as it brings him under the influence of the Spirit of God by whom he is rendered righteous. This is so repugnant to the above doctrine that it can never be reconciled with it.[17]

These are fighting words. The Reformation debate took place more in the arena of sharp polemics than in irenic negotiation. Calvin throws down the gauntlet here. Are we justified by the *imputed* righteousness of Christ or by the righteousness of Christ that becomes *inherent* in the believer, by infused grace or imputed grace? Calvin says that the difference between being righteous by imputation and being "rendered" righteous is one that "can never be reconciled."

Of course those who hold these disparate views can be reconciled if one or the other changes his position. Otherwise the two views can never be reconciled because they are mutually exclusive.

A Legal Fiction?

Rome rejects this concept of imputed, forensic justification on the grounds that it involves God in a "legal fiction." Rome alleges that this view casts a shadow on the integrity of God and his justice. For God to consider someone just who is not inherently just is for God to be guilty of some sort of fictional deceit. Rome cannot tolerate Luther's *simul iustus et peccator*. A person is either just or sinful; one cannot be both at the same time. (For the

Reformers one is both at the same *time* but not in the same *sense*.) For Rome only the inherently just can be declared just by God.

Rome's view presupposes that the only *true* justness or righteousness is inherent righteousness. It denies the truth of imputation. The biblical doctrine of justification is not a legal fiction. It is a legal reality precisely because it is based on a real (or true) imputation of real and true righteousness. Neither Christ's righteousness nor its imputation to us is a matter of fiction. It represents the reality of divine grace. G. C. Berkouwer says: ". . . the correlation between faith and grace excludes the fiction."[18] James Buchanan observes:

> The imputation of sin and righteousness is not "a legal fiction," if by that expression be meant anything that is unreal or untrue. We make this statement with a limitation, because there are some "legal fictions," so called, which are very far from being unreal. It is "a legal fiction" to say, that "the king can do no wrong"; for unquestionably in his private and personal capacity he can commit sin, and may even be guilty of crime; but in his public and official capacity, as the head of the State, he is held in the law of this country to be irresponsible; and the errors or crimes of the government are imputed to his constitutional advisers, who are regarded and treated, by reason of their official position, as alone answerable for them.[19]

Perhaps the charge of legal fiction is the most serious and grievous charge leveled against the Reformation and *sola fide*. Nothing less than the gospel is at stake. The charge of legal fiction makes the gospel itself a fiction. The biblical gospel stands or falls with the concept of imputation. Without the imputation of our sins to Christ, there is no atonement. Without the imputation of Christ's righteousness to us, all the infused grace we have will not save us. Christians who receive the grace of regeneration and the indwelling presence and power of the Holy Spirit still sin and fall short of the glory of God.

All the benefits of sacramental grace, as powerful and effective as they are claimed to be, do not gain us the holiness required by absolute justice. We need a greater righteousness than whatever righteousness inheres in us, by whatever means of grace it so inheres, in order to stand before God's judgment.

It is for this reason that Martin Luther and the Reformers insisted that the righteousness by which we are justified is an *iustitia extra nos*, a "righteousness outside of or apart from us," imputed to us.

When Luther spoke of this righteousness *extra nos*, he understood that the *extra* becomes ours in the sight of God by faith. Again, the focus is on the *grounds* of our justification. The righteousness by which I am declared righteous is one that was achieved and merited before I was even born. It is the righteousness of "another," even Jesus Christ the Righteous. His righteousness is not my righteousness intrinsically. It becomes mine only by forensic imputation. It is a righteousness that counts for me and is reckoned to my account, but it was neither achieved nor wrought by me.

In like manner Luther argued that the righteousness providing the ground of our justification is an *iustitia alienum*, an "alien righteousness." This is the righteousness of another, one who is a "foreigner" to us. He is foreign to us, not in the sense that he is unknown by us or that he remains a mysterious stranger to us, but in the sense that he is ever and always distinguishable from us, even though by faith we are "in" him and he is "in" us.

James Buchanan links the righteousness of Christ to the biblical concept of the divine righteousness by which we are justified: " . . . these two—God's righteousness which was declared, and Christ's righteousness which was wrought out, on the Cross—although they may be distinguished, cannot be separated. . . ."[20] Buchanan goes on to affirm: " . . . the righteousness of Christ, considered as the merit of His Mediatorial work, must ever continue, even when it is imputed to us, to belong primarily, and, in one important respect, exclusively, to Him by whom alone that work was accomplished. It is His righteousness in a sense in which it never can be ours: it is His, as having been wrought out by Him; and it is ours, only as it is imputed to us."[21]

Again we see that the Reformation doctrine of justification by faith alone means in its essence that we are justified by Christ and his righteousness alone, a righteousness imputed to us by faith.

Rome does not deny that we are justified by the righteousness of Christ. As we will explore in greater detail later, Rome sees the righteousness of Christ as a necessary condition for our justification. The issue remains, How is that righteousness appropriated by the believer? For Rome the righteousness of Christ is not *imputed to* the believer, but *infused into* the believer. When the believer cooperates with this infused righteousness, the believer then possesses an inherent righteousness, which then becomes the ground of justification. At this point the righteousness by which we are justified is neither *extra nos* nor an alien righteousness.

Analytical and Synthetic Views

To clarify the nature of forensic justification, Reformed theology distinguishes between an *analytical* view of justification (the Roman Catholic view) and a *synthetic* view (the Reformation view).

Linguistic philosophy differentiates sharply between analytical and synthetic statements. An analytical statement is basically a tautology or redundancy. It is true by definition or by analysis. Nothing is added in the predicate that is not already inherent in the subject.

For example, "A triangle is a three-sided figure" or "A bachelor is an unmarried man." The verb *is* functions as a copula linking identical concepts. A triangle by definition has three sides. A bachelor by definition is an unmarried man. There is no such thing as a married bachelor. If we analyze the term *bachelor,* we realize that it refers inherently to an unmarried man.

The mathematical formula $2 + 2 = 4$ is also analytical. Both sides of the equation are equal to the other. The "4" of the predicate contains no new information missing from the subject.

A synthetic statement, on the other hand, adds information in the predicate that is not inherent in the subject. The proposition

"The bachelor is bald" says something about the bachelor that is not true of all bachelors and therefore not inherent in the concept of bachelorness. There is a kind of synthesis between bachelorness and baldness. The concept of baldness is *added* to the concept of bachelorness in this specific instance. One particular from the universal category of bachelorness is combined with another particular trait of humanness, namely baldness.

The Roman Catholic view of justification is analytical in that God declares a person to be just when justice (or righteousness) inheres in the subject. The subject, under divine analysis or scrutiny, is found to be just. God justifies the just. The justified person could not have become righteous without the assistance of infused grace, but he is still deemed righteous only when he has become inherently righteous. Nothing is added by which the person is considered righteous. The just are declared just because analysis demonstrates that they are just.

By stark and radical contrast the Reformation view of justification is synthetic. God declares a person just based on something that is added, something that is not inherent in the person: the imputed righteousness of Christ. The gracious character of our justification stands out in bold relief, revealing that God is both just and the justifier of those who believe. G. C. Berkouwer observes: "But in the declaratory character of justification lies the constant reminder of the pure correlation between grace and faith."[22]

Berkouwer maintains that both *sola fide* and *sola gratia* find their purest expression in forensic justification.

McGrath on Justification

Alister McGrath notes four characteristics of the Protestant doctrine of justification that were firmly established by the year 1540:

1. Justification is the forensic *declaration* that the Christian is righteous, rather than the process by which he or she is *made* righteous. It involves a change in *status* rather than in *nature.*

2. A deliberate and systematic distinction is made between justification (the external act by which God declares the believer to be righteous) and sanctification or regeneration (the internal process of renewal by the Holy Spirit).

3. Justifying righteousness is the alien righteousness of Christ, imputed to the believer and external to him, not a righteousness that is inherent within him, located within him, or in any way belonging to him.

4. Justification takes place *per fidem propter Christum*, with faith being understood as the God-given means of justification and the merits of Christ the God-given foundation of justification.[23]

McGrath's summary of the issues is not without its problems. In his first point regarding forensic justification, he says, "It involves a change in status rather than in nature." What does McGrath mean by *involves*? Technically, as we have seen, the term *justification* does refer to the judicial declaration of God about the person who receives the benefit of this declaration and is said to be justified. The *declaration* implies the changed status of the believer. The declaration does not itself change the believer's nature. As John Gerstner relentlessly points out, however, the declaration is not directed toward people who are unchanged in their constituent nature. God does not declare a change in status of people who are unchanged in nature.

Justification, technically considered, may not *mean* the change of human nature, but it certainly *implies* a change in nature. This slip of the pen may be unintended by McGrath since in his second point he deliberately distinguishes "between justification . . . and sanctification or regeneration," both of which do effect a change in the believer.

It is proper to distinguish between justification and sanctification, but we must not separate them. They are intimately *involved* with one another. Indeed, if sanctification and regeneration are not involved, there is no justification. Faith and justification must be distinguished, but faith is *involved* in our justification as its instrumental cause. Causes and effects are distinguished, but they are involved with each other in what may be called the "causal nexus."

In this sense we may speak of the *complex* or *nexus* of *justification*. In the narrow sense *justification* refers strictly to God's forensic declaration. But in the complex of justification—its wider sense—other elements are involved. This is important to maintain if we are to avoid the antinomian error of assuming that God justifies people who are and remain unchanged.

Regeneration is a vital change in a person's nature. All who possess saving faith are regenerate. This means simply that all who are justified are also regenerate. They have been changed in their nature but are by no means perfected.

It is not the change in our nature wrought by regeneration or even the faith that flows from it that is the ground of our justification. That remains solely the imputed righteousness of Christ. The point is simply that the righteousness of Christ is not imputed to unregenerate or unbelieving persons. John Gerstner comments:

> Just as there are Protestants, as well as Romanists, who misunderstand historic Protestant justification, so there are Romanists who do understand it. Thus Michael Root . . . has stated that according to "every Reformation theologian I know, . . . coming to faith in the justifying righteousness of Christ constitutes a momentous change in the believer." By contrast, Alister McGrath, in his two-volume survey of justification, says that Protestants understand justification as "*strictly*" a legal declaration of righteousness which works no "real change" in the believer.[24]

Earlier Gerstner cites a similar reference by Kenneth Foreman: "[Justification] does not refer to the state of man, only to his status." Here Gerstner says, "True, it does not 'refer to the state of man,' but it does not exclude it."[25]

Perhaps this point can be clarified by noting the difference between the words *strictly* and *merely*. When McGrath says that justification is *strictly* a legal declaration of righteousness, he is technically correct if he is not suggesting that it is *merely* a legal declaration, with no real and momentous change occurring in the sinner.

After his analysis of justification, McGrath concludes:

> On the basis of the above analysis, it will be clear that there exist real differences between Protestants and Roman Catholics over the matter of justification. The question remains, however, as to the significance of these differences. How important, for example, is the distinction between an alien and an intrinsic justifying righteousness? In recent years, there appears to be increasing sympathy for the view that these differences, although of importance in the Reformation period, no longer possess the significance that they once had. This is not to say that the Christian denominations are agreed on the matter of justification, for it is obvious that their respective teachings have a very different "feel" or "atmosphere" to them. It seems that in the modern period the Christian denominations have preferred to concentrate on their points of agreement, rather than draw attention to their historical disagreements!
>
> This may be due in part to an increasing recognition that today the real threat to the gospel of grace comes from the rationalism of the Enlightenment rather than from other Christian denominations.[26]

This shocking summary, written before ECT appeared in 1994, makes McGrath appear like a prophet. He suggests that the distinction between alien and intrinsic righteousness, which the Reformers believed to be of utmost significance, is not that significant to modern Protestants. He is correct in his historical assessment that in recent years Protestants have weakened their view of the importance of the matter. ECT makes that abundantly clear.

He goes on to suggest that the "real threat" to the gospel comes out of the rationalism of the Enlightenment.

Does this mean that the Roman denial of *sola fide* is not a "real" threat to the gospel? I can imagine no Reformed theologian from the sixteenth century to the present day suggesting that the Roman Catholic view is not a real threat to the gospel. If the gospel is the announcement of *sola fide,* as the Reformers believed, and if *sola fide* with its stress on the imputation of Christ's righteousness is essential to the gospel, then any denial of it is certainly a threat to it. No doubt Enlightenment views are also a threat to the gospel. It would be a luxury if the gospel were assailed from only one direction and there were only one "real" or "significant" threat to it, but that is not the case.

It would be wonderful if the threat of secular modernity would bring Rome and the Reformers together, but that cannot happen unless there is real and substantive agreement on the very nature of the gospel. The threat of new opposition must not incite us to negotiate away the gospel in order to resolve long-standing issues.

The issue of justification by the imputation of Christ's righteousness was deemed significant in the sixteenth century because it was a struggle about understanding, believing, and teaching the first-century gospel. Now, more than ever, precisely because of the pervasive influence of secular modernity, the church needs a clear understanding of the biblical gospel.

It is not us that these Tridentine Fathers anathematize so much as Paul, to whom we owe the definition that the righteousness of man consists in the forgiveness of sins.

John Calvin

Infused Righteousness:
The Catholic Doctrine

What is the Roman Catholic view of justification? It would seem to be an easy matter to answer this question. Rome is a confessional body. Her doctrines are spelled out clearly in papal encyclicals and conciliar decrees. A compendium of such official teaching may be found in Heinrich Denzinger's *Enchiridion Symbolorum*.

Just as historic Protestant churches have codified their faith by such confessional documents as the Augsburg Confession, the Westminster Confession, and the Belgic Confession, so Rome has set forth her views in such historical documents.

What seems simple at first sight, however, becomes more complex when we take a second glance at the question. Not all Protestants who belong to various denominations believe in or adhere to their church's confessional standards. Despite confessional positions, theologians continue to debate doctrines that were supposedly "settled" by earlier historical decisions. Within

Protestantism such ongoing dispute reflects the precept of *semper reformanda*, "always reforming" and correcting past errors. Protestant creeds are not hampered by a commitment to any form of ecclesiastical infallibility.

On the other hand Rome, with her infallibility decree at Vatican I and in *Pastor aeternus* (1870), has a bigger problem with introducing change into dogmatic formulations. Though some sort of change may be introduced, the change may not be construed as a *correction* of former error. Here Rome suffers from a kind of theological hemophilia—scratch her and she bleeds to death.

Expanding and Clarifying

That Rome does at times change is beyond dispute. It is the manner and mode of the change that is problematic. The concept of change is involved with what Hans Küng calls *Dogmenentwicklung*, the "development of dogma." This allows for expansion and clarification. In every age the church faces different cultural pressures and issues. The *Zeitgeist* (spirit of the age) always conditions the formulations of that age. Küng notes: "Most dogmatic definitions are *polemical formulae*, declared against heresies, defenses against errors. . . ."[1]

The historical situation in which heresy assaults the church affects to some degree the manner in which the church responds. Perhaps the most vivid example of this is the pivotal "*homo-ousios*" formula included in the Nicene Creed in A.D. 325.

That Christ is of "one essence" or "cosubstantial" with the Father was crucial to the church's confession of the Trinity and of the deity of Christ. This was a resounding no to the Arian heresy, dynamic monarchianism or adoptionism. To support their heresy the followers of Arius sought refuge in an earlier formulation at Antioch in A.D. 268. At Antioch the term *homo-ousios* (same substance) was rejected and their term *homoi-ousios* (similar substance) was embraced. The Arians were willing to say that Christ had a "like" or "similar" essence, nature, or substance to that of the Father, but they denied the trinitarian view that Christ and the Father have an identity of being. The Arians accused the Trinitarians of departing from the orthodoxy established in 268 at Antioch.

Did the church change at Nicea in 325? Did Nicea correct Antioch? By no means. The historical framework of the debate in 325 was radically different from the situation in 268. By 325 the church faced a different heresy. At Antioch the enemy was the Sabellian heresy, which used the term *homo-ousios* to support a gnostic view of Christ: Christ was of the same essence as God, but he was a lower being than God. Here *homo-ousios* was used in a *modalistic sense* (modalistic monarchianism) to deny full deity to Christ.

The church at both Antioch and Nicea sought to affirm Christ's full deity. The church did not "correct" Antioch at Nicea. Two different heresies were in view at two different times. On each occasion the church articulated its trinitarian faith. At Antioch it opposed the Sabellians, who interpreted *homo-ousios* one way, and at Nicea it opposed the Arians, who interpreted *homo-ousios* in another way.

A second example of the church modifying doctrine concerns the famous formula introduced by Cyprian: *Extra ecclesiam nulla salus* (Outside the church there is no salvation). Cyprian, bishop of Carthage in the third century, also declared that one cannot have God as Father if one does not have the church as one's mother (*habere non potest Deum patrem, qui ecclesiam non habet matrem*).[2] In Cyprian's terms it is as necessary to be in the Catholic Church to be saved as it was to be in Noah's ark to survive the flood.

This narrow and restrictive view of being *within* the church as opposed to being "outside" (*extra*) the church underwent gradual development. In 1441 the Council of Florence declared that those who are not in the church are heathens, Jews, schismatics, and heretics, and they have no part in eternal life. This strict view was reiterated at Vatican I, where the Roman Church was described as the only sheepfold with but one Shepherd. This view was reaffirmed by Pius XII in the encyclicals *Mystici corporis Christi* (1943) and *Humani generis* (1950).

The *extra ecclesiam* formula has, however, undergone certain modifications of significance. Before Vatican I Pius IX issued *allocutiones* (1854) in which he said those who are outside the church because of *invincible ignorance* can still be saved. He distinguished between the ignorant (*ignorantia*) and the pertinacious (*pertinacia*).[3]

Another subtle but crucial distinction developed as well. At Trent the translation of the sinner to the state of grace was said to be "through the laver of regeneration *or its desire. . . .*"[4] This clause allows for exceptional instances when a person who desires baptism but for some reason is unable to receive it is considered to be baptized into the communion of the church. The same distinction was added in the case of one who desires to unite with the church (*votum ecclesiae*) but is prevented by circumstances from doing so. This person has an *explicit* desire to join the church (*votum explicitum*). This was further modified by the encyclical *Mystici corporis Christi* (1943), in which an implicit desire for the church is acknowledged in those who earnestly desire to do the will of God. This is the *votum ecclesiae implicitum*,[5] which greatly broadens the scope of the *extra ecclesiam*.

We see then that Rome is capable of broadening and developing its doctrine. The historical development of the *extra ecclesiam* formula does not involve its repeal, repudiation, or denial. It is *expanded* as Rome broadens its understanding of what it means to be "inside" or "outside" the church.

Because such developments clearly take place, many contemporary thinkers have a sanguine view about Rome's retreating from Trent's condemnation of *sola fide*. The language Rome uses today to describe those "separated brethren" within Protestantism is heard as a tacit denial of the anathemas of Trent, as a softening or even changing of Rome's view of justification.

Trent: A Terminal Council?

The question before us is this: Is the Council of Trent's teaching on justification the church's final word? Emphatically not.

Rome has developed its doctrine of justification, and it will doubtless continue to do so. None of the ecumenical councils, not even Chalcedon or Nicea, is terminal in the sense that it ends all possible development.

They are not terminal, but *they are decisive*. Rome can indeed develop the views expressed at Trent. What it cannot do without radically altering its view of itself is repudiate or "correct" Trent. Those who look for such a repudiation, or who think they have already found it, are whistling in the dark.

Rome's view of justification vis-à-vis the Protestant view was set forth at Trent, particularly during the sixth session.

At this council Rome went to great lengths to distance herself from the ancient heresies of Pelagius, who had been condemned at the second Synod of Orange.[6] Pelagius had argued that Adam's sin affected Adam alone and was not transferred or imputed to his posterity via original sin. Man is capable of being righteous without grace, though grace "facilitates" righteousness.

At Trent Rome clearly and strongly affirmed the necessity of grace for salvation. Though the Reformation debate over merit and grace was crucial, as we will see later, at no point did Rome deny the necessity of grace.

In like manner Trent emphasized the necessity of faith for justification. Trent declares: ". . .we are therefore said to be justified by faith, because faith is the beginning of human salvation, the foundation and root of all justification, 'without which it is impossible to please God' (Heb. 11:6) and to come to the fellowship of His sons; and we are therefore said to be justified gratuitously, because none of those things that precede justification, whether faith or works, merit the grace of justification."[7]

Far from excluding faith as a necessary condition for justification, Rome declares faith is a necessary ingredient of justification. This declaration says several important things about faith: (1) justification is by faith (*per fidem*), (2) faith is the "beginning" (*initium)* of salvation, (3) faith is the "foundation" (*fundamentum*) of all justification, and (4) faith is the "root" (*radix*) of all justification.[8]

We conclude that when Rome speaks of justification *by* faith, she means at least that faith is the beginning, foundation, and root of all justification. If we play a bit with the Latin terms here, we could say that faith is the initial, fundamental, and radical to justification.

However this is understood, it is clear that Rome does affirm some sort of justification by faith. What Rome affirms, however, differs dramatically from the Reformation view of justification by faith. Most obvious is Rome's exclusion of the word *alone* (*sola*). Martin Luther and the Reformers insisted that justification is by faith alone. Rome affirms that justification is "by faith," but not "by faith alone."

A second critical difference involves the meaning of the term *by* (*per*). For the Reformers *by* refers to faith as the instrumental cause of justification or the means by which it is appropriated. As we have seen, the Reformers saw the righteousness or merit of Christ as being the sole grounds of our justification, and Christ's righteousness is imputed to the believer *by* faith. Faith then is the instrument or instrumental cause by which the believer is linked to Christ and his righteousness forensically.

Rome does not use *by* in the same sense. This is clear when Rome insists that the instrumental cause of justification is the sacrament of baptism. Baptism is the *primary* instrumental cause of justification in that it is the first or initial cause of justification. Since the grace of justification received by baptism may be lost, the *secondary* instrumental cause of justification is the sacrament of penance. In chapter 14 of Trent's sixth session, we read: "Those who through sin have forfeited the received grace of justification, can again be justified when, moved by God, they exert themselves to obtain through the sacrament of penance the recovery, by the merits of Christ, of the grace lost. For this manner of justification is restoration for those fallen, which the holy Fathers have aptly called a second plank after the shipwreck of grace lost."[9]

For Rome, then, faith is not the instrumental cause of justification. That cause is the sacraments, in the first instance baptism, and in the second, restorative sense, penance. The new *Catechism of the Catholic Church* declares: "Justification is conferred in Baptism, the sacrament of faith. It conforms us to the righteousness of God, who makes us inwardly just by the power of his mercy."[10] Baptism *confers* justification and in that sense it is the instrumental cause of justification.

That justification is not by faith alone is made crystal clear by chapter 15 of Trent's sixth session:

> Against the subtle wits of some also, who "by pleasing speeches and good words seduce the hearts of the innocent" (Rom. 16:18), it must be maintained that the grace of justification once received is lost not only by infidelity, whereby also faith itself is lost, but also by every other mortal sin, though in this case faith is not lost; thus defending the teaching of the divine law which excludes from the kingdom of God not only unbelievers, but also the faithful [who are] "fornicators, adulterers, effeminate, liers with mankind, thieves, covetous, drunkards, railers, extortioners" (1 Cor. 6:9f.; 1 Tim. 1:9f.), and all others who commit deadly sins, from which with the help of divine grace they can refrain, and on account of which they are cut off from the grace of Christ.[11]

This statement raises serious ancillary issues that divide Rome from historic Protestantism, such as the possibility of falling from a state of grace, and an implicit (if not explicit) antinomianism. But our concern here is the relationship of faith and justification.

Trent indicates that the grace of justification can be lost in two ways. The first is by infidelity, in which case faith is lost and justification with it. The second and more significant way is by mortal sin, in which case one may have faith but lose justification. If it is possible to have true faith but not have justification, then it is clear, by resistless logic, that justification is not by faith alone. Again it is arguable whether such faith would be considered true faith by the Reformers. Yet it is considered true faith by Rome, and this faith does not include justification.

Returning now to Rome's view of faith as the foundation and root of justification and to her declaration that justification is by faith, we see that *by* does not mean that faith is the "instrumental" cause of justification. What does *by* mean?

To answer this question we must first determine what *by* does not mean. Clearly Rome is saying that justification is not *without* or *apart from* faith. Faith remains the necessary foundation and root of justification. For Rome justification by faith means at least that justification is *with* faith and *in some sense* by or through faith. That *by* or *through* at least points to faith accompanying justification.

Calvin's Rebuttal

In the sixteenth century John Calvin responded to this declaration with sharp criticism:

> Seeing that the doctrine of Scripture was obviously repugnant to their decrees, they, to prevent this from being suspected, first explain what it is for a man to be justified by faith, saying, that faith is the beginning of salvation, and the foundation of justification. As if they had disentangled themselves by this solution, they immediately fly off to another—that the Apostle teaches that we are justified freely, because all the things which precede justification, whether faith or works, do not merit it. . . . Faith justifies, since it *begins* justification.[12]

Calvin then reviewed the biblical teaching on justification, particularly Paul's use of Abraham as the exemplar of those justified by faith:

> Faith therefore does not open up an access to him to righteousness, in order that his justification may afterwards be completed elsewhere. . . . As far as a fixed and immovable station is from a transient passage, so far are they in this dogma of theirs from the meaning of Paul. To collect all the passages of Scripture were tedious and superfluous. From these few, I presume, it is already superabundantly clear, that the completion, not less than the commencement of justification, must be ascribed to faith.[13]

In the heat of Calvin's polemic the issue of faith's role in justification becomes clear. For Rome faith is the *beginning* of justification, but this beginning does not yield permanent justification. Calvin made it "superabundantly clear" that justification in its *completion* as well as its *initiation* should be ascribed to faith.

The chief reason Calvin ascribed to faith the completion of justification is that justification rests on the imputation of Christ's righteousness to the believer. What is required for our justification is the imputation of Christ's righteousness, and that righteousness is imputed the moment faith is present.

This turns us back to the critical issue of justification by the *imputation* of Christ's righteousness to the believer versus justification by the *infusion* of Christ's righteousness into the believer. Since the infusion of Christ's righteousness is initiated by faith, Rome can say that justification is by faith. However, since the infusion of Christ's righteousness does not *complete* our justification immediately, we are not justified by faith alone.

The Reformation focused on the distinction between infused and imputed righteousness, as we have seen in our treatment of forensic justification. For Rome the infusion of Christ's righteousness makes justification possible if the believer assents to and cooperates with (*assentire et cooperare*) this grace. Chapter 16 of Trent declares:

> For since Christ Jesus Himself, as the head into the members and the vine into the branches (John 15:1f.), continually infuses strength into those justified, which strength always precedes, accompanies and follows their good works, and without which they could not in any manner be pleasing and meritorious before God, we must believe that nothing further is wanting to those justified to prevent them from being considered to have, by those very works which have been done in God, fully satisfied the divine law according to the state of this life and to have truly merited eternal life. . . .[14]

Here Rome appeals to the New Testament metaphor of Christ as the vine, the source of strength for the branches. It is the infusion of his righteousness into the believer that provides the strength necessary to perform good works. Trent emphatically declares that this infused strength always "precedes, accompanies and follows" the believer's good works. This infused strength does not merely precede, accompany, or follow good works; it is the *sine qua non* of good works.

Again it is clear that Trent seeks to distance itself from any crass form of Pelagianism. The graciously infused righteousness of Christ is absolutely necessary for justification. This is emphatically not a doctrine of *self*-righteousness. Trent declares that without this infusion the good works of the believer could not "in any manner be pleasing and meritorious before God."

In *Evangelicals and Catholics Together* the united affirmation of justification reads: "We affirm together that we are justified by grace through faith because of Christ."[15] This statement is consistent with the Tridentine view of justification. Justification rests on grace. It comes through faith (*per fidem*). And it is "because of Christ," in that without the infused righteousness of Christ it could not occur.

Protestants and Roman Catholics can easily agree on this joint affirmation—as far as it goes. The orthodox Catholic would interpret it à la Trent. The orthodox Evangelical would interpret it to mean something else. For a Catholic "because of Christ" points to the *infusion* of Christ's righteousness by which a person becomes just. For the Evangelical "because of Christ" points to the *imputation* of Christ's righteousness by which a person is declared just.

Trent further affirms in chapter 16 that the infused strength of Christ is not only *necessary* for justification, but also (when and if the believer cooperates with it) efficacious in achieving justification. By virtue of the fruit of this infused strength (i.e., good works), nothing further is needed to fully satisfy divine law and truly merit eternal life.

Chapter 16 continues: "Thus, neither is our own justice established as our own from ourselves (Rom. 10:3; 2 Cor. 3:5), nor is the justice of God ignored or repudiated, for that justice which is called ours, because we are justified by its inherence in us, that same is [the justice] of God, because it is infused into us by God through the merit of Christ."[16]

Rome seeks to steer a course between Pelagian self-righteousness and the Reformation view that Rome considers a legal fiction. In the first instance it declares that our own justice is not established as our own from ourselves. In the second instance it does not ignore or repudiate the justice of God. It respects the justice of God in two ways: (1) our justification rests on divine justice because it comes to us from God via infusion, and (2) God declares just those who now have *inherent* justice or righteousness.

The difference between the Roman Catholic doctrine of justification and that of the Reformers is most crucial at the point of issue between imputed and infused righteousness. Chapter 16 ends with a most solemn declaration: "After this Catholic doctrine on justification, which whosoever does not faithfully and firmly accept cannot be justified, it seemed good to the holy council to add these canons, that all may know not only what they must hold and follow, but also what to avoid and shun."[17]

This final paragraph of chapter 16 serves as a transition from an exposition of the Tridentine doctrine of justification to the canons condemning views that depart from it.

Rome solemnly declares that if a person does not "*faithfully and firmly accept*" this doctrine, he "cannot be justified." To embrace the Roman Catholic doctrine of justification (and to do so faithfully and firmly) is itself a necessary condition for justification. At this point Rome affirms that her doctrine of justification is an essential article of the faith, essential to salvation itself. The Reformers were equally firm in their insistence that something essential to salvation is at stake here.

Three Canons

After articulating the doctrine of justification by infused righteousness and declaring that acceptance of this doctrine is necessary for justification, Trent declared in canon 11: "If anyone says that men are justified either by the sole imputation of the justice of Christ or by the sole remission of sins, to the exclusion of the grace and 'the charity which is poured forth in their hearts by the Holy Ghost' (Rom. 5:5), and remains in them, or also that the grace by which we are justified is only the good will of God, let him be anathema."[18]

This canon is something of a shotgun blast. Some of its pellets missed the Reformation position completely, while others hit home. The Reformers did not exclude the infusion of grace from the justified sinner. Indeed grace is poured into the soul via regeneration and the indwelling of the Holy Spirit. The issue was the ground of our justification. For the Reformers the ground of our justification is the imputed righteousness of Christ, not the infused righteousness of Christ that inheres in the believer.

The shotgun does blast the Reformed doctrine of imputation. The Reformers did say we are justified by the sole imputation of the justice of Christ, but they did not say that this imputation excludes the infusion of grace into the believer. Nor did the Reformers teach that justification is "only" the good will of God.

The final clause misses the point. It hits the Socinian view of justification, a view as repugnant to the Reformers as it was to Rome.

Calvin responded sharply to canon 11:

> I wish the reader to understand that as often as we mention Faith alone in this question, we are not thinking of a dead faith, which worketh not by love, but holding faith to be the only cause of justification (Gal. 5:6; Rom. 3:22). It is therefore faith alone which justifies, and yet the faith which justifies is not alone: just as it is the heat alone of the sun which warms the earth, and yet in the sun it is not alone, because it is constantly conjoined with light. Wherefore we do not separate the whole grace of regeneration from faith, but claim the power and faculty of justifying entirely for faith, as we ought. And yet it is not us that these Tridentine Fathers anathematize so much as Paul, to whom we owe the definition that the righteousness of man consists in the forgiveness of sins.[19]

Just as canon 11 suffers from imprecision, so do canons 9 and 10.

Canon 9 declared: "If anyone says that the sinner is justified by faith alone, meaning that nothing else is required to cooperate in order to obtain the grace of justification, and that it is not in any way necessary that he be prepared and disposed by the action of his own will, let him be anathema."[20]

To this statement Calvin responded:

> This Canon is very far from being canonical; for it joins things which are utterly at variance. They imagine that a man is justified by faith without any movement of his own will, as if it were not with the heart that a man believeth unto righteousness. Between them and us there is this difference, that they persuade themselves that the movement comes from the man himself, whereas we maintain that faith is voluntary, because God draws our wills to himself. Add, that when we say a man is justified by faith alone, we do not fancy a faith devoid of charity, but we mean that faith alone is the cause of justification.[21]

The point of Calvin's response is to duck the scatter-blast of this canon. Though Calvin and the Reformers insisted that justification is by faith alone, they did not mean that human volition is absent from the nexus of faith. The *sola fide* anathematized by canon 9 is not the *sola fide* of the Reformation. Saving faith is not devoid of will or of charity, but neither the sinner's volition nor his exercise of charity is the "cause" of justification.

Canon 10 of Trent raises serious questions about the forensic character of justification: "If anyone says that men are justified without the justice of Christ (Gal. 2:16), whereby He merited for us, or by that justice are formally just, let him be anathema."[22]

This brief canon is somewhat confusing. The first clause condemns the idea that we can be justified without the justice of Christ that he merited for us. This clearly condemns the Pelagian heresy of justification apart from the righteousness of Christ. Both Rome and the Reformers insisted that justification is by the righteousness of Christ. As we have already seen, the issue raged over *how* the righteousness of Christ avails for our justification. Is it the righteousness of Christ imputed to us, or is it the righteousness of Christ infused within us?

The final clause of canon 10 gets to the heart of the issue. This clause condemns not only Pelagianism but also *formal justification.* Obviously in view here is the distinction between *formal justification* and *material justification.* This distinction finds its impetus in classic theological language, with its roots in Aristotle's distinction between form and matter. The difference between the formal and the material has to do with the difference between the essential and the existential, the conceptual and the real, the cognitive and the empirical.

For the Reformers, believers are *formally just* in the sense that God considers, counts, or reckons them just when in themselves they are not existentially, really, or empirically just. This does not mean that justification is a "mere formality," a legal fiction. When God formally considers a person righteous, he does so on the basis of a *real imputation* of the *real righteousness* of Christ. For Rome (which also speaks of divine justice as the "single formal cause" of justification), God's formal declaration of justification rests on the believer's *material* righteousness.

Rome's condemnation of "formal" justification had in view the Lutheran and Reformed view that the believer is *simul iustus et peccator*. The Reformers asserted that God considers the believer formally just before he is materially just. For Rome God does not consider the believer formally just until or unless he is materially just.

Calvin responds to canon 10:

> Could these anathemas take effect, all who are not versed in the sophistical art would pay dearly for their simplicity. They formerly asserted in their decrees that the righteousness of God was the only formal cause of Justification; now they anathematize those who say that we are formally righteous by the obedience of Christ. . . . For as it were impious to say that the righteousness of Christ is only an exemplar or type to us, so if any one were to teach that we are righteous formally, *i.e.*, not by quality but by imputation, meaning that our righteousness is in relation merely, there would be nothing worthy of censure. The adverb *formally* is used in both senses.[23]

Many of the remaining canons of the sixth session of Trent speak about the function of works in justification and about the assurance of salvation. These matters were sharply debated during the Reformation but will not be considered here.

The relationships between merit and grace and between faith and works are such important issues to the broader question of justification that we will treat them separately in subsequent chapters.

The Council of Trent closed with a petition for papal confirmation of the canons and decrees it had enacted. This petition was heard and granted by Pius IV. In confirming Trent Pius declared:

> Moreover, in virtue of holy obedience and under the penalties prescribed by the holy canons, and others more severe, even of deprivation, to be imposed at our discretion, we command each and all of our venerable brethren, patriarchs, archbishops, bishops, and all other prelates of churches, whatever may be their state, rank, order and dignity, even though distinguished with the honor of the cardinalate, to observe diligently the said decrees and ordinances in their churches, cities and dioceses both in and out of the court of justice, and to cause them to be observed inviolately, each by his own subjects whom it may in any way concern; restraining all opponents and obstinate persons by means of judicial sentences, censures and ecclesiastical penalties contained in those decrees, every appeal being set aside, calling in also, if need be, the aid of the secular arm.[24]

There is no such thing as merit;
but all who are justified
are justified for nothing (gratis),
and this is credited to no one
but to the grace of God. . . .
For Christ alone it is proper
to help and save others
with His merits and works.

Martin Luther

7

Merit and Grace

In addition to *sola fide* and *sola Scriptura*, the Reformers stressed *sola gratia*, "by grace alone." The gracious character of salvation was affirmed both by Rome and by the Reformers, together appealing to the great St. Augustine.

The concept of *sola gratia* in historical theology originated in the fierce controversy of the fifth century over the Pelagian heresy. Before we examine the ongoing issue of merit and grace, we will briefly summarize that debate.

Augustine and Pelagius

The main players in the Pelagian controversy were St. Augustine on one side, and the triumvirate of the monk Pelagius, the eunuch Coelestius, and the bishop Julian of Eclanum on the other side.

Before the great controversy broke out, Pelagius had taken umbrage at Augustine's famous prayer, "Grant what thou commandest, and command what thou dost desire." Pelagius was disturbed by the idea that God must grant by grace the ability to do what he commands. Pelagius assumed that God cannot be just and command something that requires grace to perform. Responsibility assumes ability. Since man is responsible to act in perfect virtue, he must be able to act in perfect virtue. Adolf Harnack remarks: "Nature, free-will, virtue and law, these—strictly defined and made independent of the notion of God—were the catch-words of Pelagianism: self-acquired virtue is the supreme good which is followed by reward. Religion and morality lie in the sphere of the free spirit; they are won at any moment by man's own effort."[1]

At the Synod of Carthage the Pelagian views, expressed chiefly by Coelestius, were summarized:

> [Pelagius taught] that Adam was made mortal and would have died whether he had or had not sinned—that Adam's sin injured himself alone, and not the human race—[that] infants at birth are in that state in which Adam was before his falsehood—that the whole human race neither dies on account of Adam's death or falsehood, nor will rise again in virtue of Christ's resurrection—[that] the law admits men to the kingdom of heaven as well as the gospel—[that] even before the advent of our Lord there were impeccable men, *i.e.*, men without sin—that man can be without sin and can keep the divine commands easily if he will.[2]

The Pelagians clearly denied the doctrine of original sin. They did not deny the availability of grace, but they insisted grace is unnecessary for attaining a sinless life or entrance into heaven. Grace *facilitates* the achieving of righteousness, but it can be reached without it.

Pelagianism was condemned at the Synod of Carthage in 418 and at the Council of Ephesus in 431. Harnack summarizes Augustine's position vis-à-vis Pelagianism:

> Mankind is, as experience shows, a "mass of sin" [*massa peccati (perditionis)*], waited on by death, and incapable of raising itself to the good; for having revolted from God, it could no more return to him than an empty vessel could refill itself. . . . Christ by his

death removed the gulf between God and mankind—breaking the rule of the devil—so that the grace of God, which for that reason is *gratia per (propter) Christum*, could pursue its work. This free grace (*gratia gratis data*) working in the Church, is beginning, middle, and end.[3]

The Pelagian controversy settled the issue of the necessity of grace for salvation. What was not settled was the question of the degree to which grace is necessary and the full efficacy of grace.

Fig. 7.1

Councils Dealing with Pelagianism

Synod of Carthage	418	Condemned Pelagianism
Council of Ephesus	431	Condemned Pelagianism
Council of Orange	529	Condemned Semi-Pelagianism
Synod of Valence	855	
Council of Trent	1545–63	

The concept of grace developed over the course of centuries in Roman Catholic theology. St. Thomas Aquinas treated the question in depth in his *Summa theologica*. Thomas treated ten basic questions of divine grace.[4] In these he maintains the following:

1. If a man is to know any truth whatsoever, he needs divine help in order that his intellect may be moved to its act by God.
2. Human nature needs divine help in order to do or will any good.
3. In the state of pure nature man did not need a gift of grace added to his natural power, in order to love God above all things, although he did need the help of God moving him to do so. But in the state of corrupt nature he needs further help of grace, that his nature may be healed.
4. A man in the state of corrupt nature cannot fulfill all the divine commandments without healing grace.

5. A man cannot merit eternal life without grace.
6. A man cannot prepare himself for grace without the help of grace.
7. Man can in no wise rise from sin by himself without the help of grace.
8. A man can avoid sinful actions taken singly, but he cannot avoid all of them, unless through grace.
9. A gift of habitual grace is not given so that we may dispense with any further divine help, since every creature must be preserved by God in the good which it receives from him.
10. Even a man in grace needs that perseverance be given him by God.

After answering ten major questions concerning man's need for grace, St. Thomas goes on to describe the essence of God's grace: ". . . there are three things commonly meant by grace, as the word is used in ordinary speech. First, it means someone's love, as when we say that a certain soldier has the king's favour, i.e., that the king holds him in favour. Secondly, it means a gift freely given, as when we say: 'I do you this favour.' Thirdly, it means the response to a gift freely given, as when we are said to give thanks for benefits received."[5]

Aquinas then agrees with Augustine in avowing that "the name of grace signifies the remission of sins especially."

Thomas argues that grace, in a specific sense, may inhere in the soul. Grace is said to exist in the soul of the believer.

A crucial point of dispute between Rome and the Reformation concerning the work of God's grace was the efficacy of divine grace. Is grace irresistible and efficacious on its own, or is it resistible and dependent on human cooperation?

Aquinas distinguishes between *operative* and *cooperative* grace: "An operation which is part of an effect is attributed to the mover, not to the thing moved. The operation is therefore attributed to God when God is the sole mover, and when the mind is moved but not a mover. We then speak of 'operative grace.' But when the soul is not only moved but also a mover, the operation is attributed to the soul as well as to God. We then speak of 'co-operative grace.'"[6]

Fig. 7.2
Thomas Aquinas's Analysis of Grace

Operative grace	God moves the human will to will the good.
Cooperative grace	God moves the human will to will the good *and* the human will wills the good.
Prevenient grace	God heals the human soul.
Subsequent grace	God heals the human soul *and* the human soul wills the good.

St. Thomas argues that God moves the human will, which previously willed evil, to will good. Again citing Augustine, Thomas says, "He operates to make us will, and when we will, he co-operates with us that we may be made perfect."

Thomas also distinguishes between "prevenient grace" and "subsequent grace": ". . . just as grace is divided into operative and co-operative grace on account of its different effects, so is it divided into prevenient and subsequent grace on the same grounds. There are five effects of grace in us: first, that the soul is healed; second, that it wills what is good; third, that it carries out what it wills; fourth, that it perseveres in good; and fifth, that it attains to glory. Since grace causes the first effect in us, it is called prevenient in relation to the second effect."[7]

The question of the nature and efficacy of prevenient grace was a huge issue during the Reformation. Both sides argued that a work of grace "comes before justification." Regeneration is necessary for the fallen person to exercise faith. Faith is exercised by the believer, not the unregenerate person. The grace of regeneration must come before or precede faith. Both sides agreed that such prevenient grace is necessary. The issue was the *efficacy* of such grace. Aquinas seems to indicate, as did Augustine, that this grace was operative rather than cooperative, denying both Pelagianism and semi-Pelagianism, which was condemned by the Council of Orange in 529.

Trent and Semi-Pelagianism

Trent appeared, at least to the Reformers, to retreat to the semi-Pelagian position that, though the human will is weakened by the fall, it still has the spiritual power to incline itself toward grace. The following view was expounded in chapter 5 of Trent's sixth session:

> It is furthermore declared that in adults the beginning of that justification must proceed from the predisposing grace of God through Jesus Christ, that is, from His vocation, whereby, without any merits on their part, they are called; that they who by sin had been cut off from God, may be disposed through His quickening and helping grace to convert themselves to their own justification by freely assenting to and cooperating with that grace; so that, while God touches the heart of man through the illumination of the Holy Ghost, man himself neither does absolutely nothing while receiving that inspiration, since he can also reject it, nor yet is he able by his own free will and without the grace of God to move himself to justice in His sight.[8]

Here Rome makes it clear that fallen man cannot convert himself or even move himself to justice in God's sight without the aid of grace. Again Pelagianism is repudiated.

This predisposing grace, however, is *rejectable*. It is not in itself effectual. Its effectiveness depends on the fallen person's assent and cooperation. This sounds very much like semi-Pelagianism, which had been condemned at Orange. Earlier in the fifth session, which treated original sin, Trent affirmed some aspects of the decrees of Orange.

Rome has repeatedly been accused of condemning semi-Pelagianism at Orange but embracing it anew at Trent. Herman Bavinck held that "although semi-Pelagianism had been condemned by Rome, it reappeared in 'a roundabout way.'"[9] G. C. Berkouwer observed:

> Between Orange and Trent lies a long process of development, namely, scholasticism, with its elaboration of the doctrine of the

meritoriousness of good works, and the Roman system of peni-
tence. . . . Hence the situation became much more complicated
for Rome in Trent than when, in 529, semi-Pelagianism had to be
condemned for its "weakening" of grace. . . . Trent had to ward off
the Reformers' attack without derogating from the decrees of
Orange. . . . The *gratia praeveniens* had to be taught without relaps-
ing into the *sola fide* of the Reformers. That is why the Orange texts
are repeated in Trent, especially in the decree on justification.[10]

The Council of Trent tried to steer a course on the razor's edge
between semi-Pelagianism and Reformed thought. It is arguable
that they cut themselves on that razor. At issue was the residual
power of man's weakened, fallen will. Rome tried to argue that
the will is weaker than semi-Pelagianism allowed, but not as weak
as the Reformers insisted. Berkouwer concludes: "At Trent there
is no concern with the threat to grace as there was at Orange. But
Trent is concerned with the natural freedom of will. The latter, it
is true, has been weakened by sin (Orange, Valence, Trent) but
not at all extinguished."[11]

This issue was covered in Martin Luther's dispute with Eras-
mus in *Bondage of the Will,* as well as in John Calvin's writings.
Berkouwer remarks about Calvin: "It becomes perfectly clear why
Calvin fights the idea of free will. He does not do so from deter-
ministic considerations in which human freedom would be can-
celled by 'constraint.' On the contrary, he acknowledges that it is
an excellent thing when it is stated that man has a free will. Such
is not meant in the sense that man is free to choose either good
or evil, but in the sense that man does evil according to his own
will and is not under constraint."[12]

To avoid the Reformation and Augustinian view of the enslaved
will, Rome speaks of the power of fallen man to assent to and
cooperate with prevenient grace. That grace is not effectual without the sinner's response. As the new *Catechism of the Catholic
Church* states it, "God's free initiative demands *man's free
response,* for God has created man in his image by conferring on
him, along with freedom, the power to know him and love him."[13]
The confusion between Rome's view at Orange and later deci-

sions was exaggerated in the seventeenth-century Molinist controversy.[14]

Calvin argued that Trent in effect repudiated Augustine's doctrine of *sola gratia:*

> Is this the doctrine delivered by Augustine, when he says, "Men labour to find in our will some good thing of our own not given us of God; what they can find I know not"? . . . Indeed, as he elsewhere says, "Were man left to his own will to remain under the help of God if he chooses, while God does not make him willing, among temptations so numerous and so great, the will would succumb from its own weakness. Succour, therefore, has been brought to the weakness of the human will by divine grace acting irresistibly and inseparably, that thus the will however weak might not fail."[15]

Later Calvin cites Augustine again: ". . . the motion of the Holy Spirit is so efficacious that it always begets faith."[16]

We see then that the *sola gratia* of Trent is not the *sola gratia* strenuously affirmed by Augustine and the Reformers.

A Treasury of Merit

If grace was a major concern during the Reformation, merit was even more so. Elaborate distinctions between specific kinds of merit developed during the Scholastic period. Rome spoke of merit in several ways. She distinguished between condign merit (*meritum de condigno*) and congruous merit (*meritum de congruo*).[17] In addition Rome spoke of a treasury of merit that accrues from the merit of Christ and the supererogatory merit of Mary and the saints.

Since the concept of merit was tied closely to the sacrament of penance, the indulgence controversy focused heavily on this concept.

In expounding the sacrament of penance, the *Catechism of the Catholic Church* declares: "The doctrine and practice of indulgences in the Church are closely linked to the effects of the sacrament of Penance."[18]

Rome defines an indulgence in this manner:

> "An indulgence is a remission before God of the temporal punishment due to sins whose guilt has already been forgiven, which the faithful Christian who is duly disposed gains under certain prescribed conditions through the action of the Church which, as the minister of redemption, dispenses and applies with authority the treasury of the satisfactions of Christ and the saints."
>
> "An indulgence is partial or plenary according as it removes either part or all of the temporal punishment due to sin." Indulgences may be applied to the living or the dead.[19]

Rome declares that sin has a "double consequence": eternal punishment and temporal punishment. Forgiveness involves the remission of eternal punishment, but temporal punishment remains. ". . . every sin, even venial, entails an unhealthy attachment to creatures, which must be purified either here on earth, or after death in the state called Purgatory."[20]

Charity links the faithful in heaven to those "who are expiating their sins in purgatory." Rome calls "these spiritual goods of the communion of saints the *Church's treasury.* . . ."[21]

This treasury has an infinite value based on the merits of Christ. What is strange is that the infinite value of Christ's merit is *augmented* by the merit of Mary and the saints:

> This treasury includes as well the prayers and good works of the Blessed Virgin Mary. They are truly immense, unfathomable, and even pristine in their value before God. In the treasury, too, are the prayers and good works of all the saints, all those who have followed in the footsteps of Christ the Lord and by his grace have made their lives holy and carried out the mission the Father entrusted to them. In this way they attained their own salvation and at the same time cooperated in saving their brothers in the unity of the Mystical Body.[22]

The indulgence controversy focused on the sufficiency of the merit of Christ. The Reformers viewed the redemptive work of

Christ as totally sufficient in two respects, both negative and positive. The atonement totally expiates the sin of the believer, fully satisfying the demands of God's punitive justice. The value of Christ's sacrifice satisfies all the negative judgment of God with respect to our demerits before him.

On the positive side, the perfect active obedience of Christ fulfills all righteousness, earning all the merit needed to save the believer. Nothing can be added to Christ's atonement or to his righteousness to enhance their value and merit.

The sacrament of penance and the doctrine of the treasury of merit cast a heavy shadow over the sufficiency of Christ's saving work. According to this doctrine the prayers and good works of Mary and the saints are added to the merit of Christ. In a broad sense the saints contribute to the redemption of others. The expiation of sin accomplished by Christ must be augmented by expiation in purgatory, at least to satisfy temporal guilt.

Works of Satisfaction

The sacrament of penance calls on the penitent to do works of satisfaction, which is necessary for the second plank of justification to be fulfilled. Trent decreed that "the acts of the penitent himself, namely, contrition, confession and satisfaction, constitute the matter of this sacrament, which acts, inasmuch as they are by God's institution required in the penitent for the integrity of the sacrament and for the full and complete remission of sins, are for this reason called the parts of penance."[23]

Works of satisfaction are necessary for the justification that comes via penance: ". . . the holy council declares that it is absolutely false and contrary to the word of God, that the guilt is never remitted by the Lord without the entire punishment being remitted also."[24]

Trent appeals to both Scripture and "divine tradition" for support. Rome explains why such works of satisfaction are necessary:

> And it is in keeping with divine clemency that sins be not thus pardoned us without any satisfaction, lest seizing the occasion and

considering sins as trivial and offering insult and affront to the Holy Spirit (Heb. 10:29), we should fall into graver ones. . . . For without doubt, these satisfactions greatly restrain from sin, check as it were with a bit, and make penitents more cautious and vigilant in the future; they also remove remnants of sin, and by acts of the opposite virtues destroy habits acquired by evil living.[25]

Here the pastoral and practical benefits of works of satisfaction are stressed. They are designed to assist the believer in the process of sanctification.

There is a subtle problem here because, in at least one respect, the Reformers also called for certain fruits of repentance to be performed. For example, if a man steals money from another person and then repents of that sin, his repentance, if wrought by true contrition, results in divine forgiveness. Still, the penitent is required to make restitution for the theft. The penitent may not say, "God has forgiven my sin, therefore I can keep the money I stole."

Willingness to make restitution where possible is the fruit—indeed the necessary fruit—of true contrition. The person who "repents" without such willingness exhibits *attrition* (a repentance motivated by a fear of punishment), but not true repentance marked by godly *contrition* (a godly sorrow for having offended God, coupled with a resolve to turn away from the sin).

Repentance without contrition is not genuine repentance. The subtle point, however, is that true repentance, though attended with a willingness to make restitution, brings forgiveness *before* restitution is made. Restitution "satisfies" the command of God to pay our human debts but is not the ground of our justification before God. Only the work of Christ in our behalf can serve as the ground of justification.

For Rome the penitent's works of satisfaction are done with the help of the grace of Christ: "Neither is this satisfaction which we discharge for our sins so our own as not to be through Christ Jesus; for we who can do nothing of ourselves as of ourselves, can do all things with the cooperation of Him who strengthens us (see 2 Cor. 3:5; Phil. 4:13)."[26]

Rome seeks to avoid any crass form of self-righteousness or self-justification in the Pelagian sense. Even the works of satisfaction performed by the sinner are done, not by the sinner alone, but in cooperation with the infused grace of Christ. This cooperative, synergistic work, however, does indeed yield satisfaction: ". . . the satisfaction they impose . . . [is] not only for the protection of a new life and a remedy against infirmity, but also for the atonement and punishment of past sins; for the early Fathers also believed and taught that the keys of the priests were bestowed not to loose only but also to bind (Matt. 16:19; John 20:23)."[27]

Remember that the sacrament of penance is designed to restore fallen sinners to a state of justification. For that restoration to occur, sinners must make some satisfaction and "atonement" for their sins in addition to the satisfaction and atonement offered by Christ. These works of satisfaction, though assisted by the grace of Christ, are necessary prerequisites for justification. Full justification rests on both the satisfaction rendered by Christ *and* the satisfaction rendered by the sinner in cooperation with Christ. Justification here is clearly a synergistic work.

The Merit and Satisfaction of Christ

Rome anticipates a "protest" from Protestants at this point: ". . . no Catholic ever understood that through our satisfactions the efficacy of the merit and satisfaction of our Lord Jesus Christ is either obscured or in any way diminished; but since the innovators wish to understand it so, they teach, in order to destroy the efficacy and use of satisfaction, that a new life is the best penance."[28]

Here Trent labors the point that Rome has no desire to "obscure" or "diminish" the efficacy of Christ's merit and satisfaction. But saying these words is not enough to make it so. What other conclusion can be reached than that Roman doctrine vitiates the merit and satisfaction of Christ by whose merit and satisfaction alone we are justified?

Calvin was deeply troubled by this view of satisfaction:

It is enough for me to know the two following things—first, that they devise a Repentance altogether different from that which is recommended to us in Scripture; and secondly, that they enact a condition for obtaining the remission of sins, from which he, to whom alone the power of remitting belongs, wished us to be free. . . . For they do not permit him to pardon our sins, unless it be on the condition of our performing an observance which they alone make binding.[29]

Perhaps most troubling to the Reformers was the notion that the works of satisfaction done as part of the sacrament of penance possess a kind of merit: congruous merit. Merits of congruity (*meritum de congruo*) are so-called because, though the merit achieved does not reach the level of condign merit, it is meritorious enough to make it "congruous" or "fitting" for God to reward it. Condign merit imposes a legal obligation for reward, whereas congruous merit does not. If God did not reward congrous merit, however, he would be acting in an incongruous or unfitting way.

Donald Bloesch remarks:

The Reformers stoutly challenged the Catholic conception that sinful humanity can prepare the way for justification, though always with the assistance of grace. Late medieval theology taught that even apart from prior grace works of contrition can merit justifying grace, albeit only in a loose sense. William of Ockham and Gabriel Biel spoke of merits *de congruo,* meaning that we can do works that may induce God's favor, so long as they are done in sincerity and so long as we do what in us lies. Merit in the strict sense—works that truly deserve God's favor (*de condigno*)—is not possible apart from His assisting grace. The Council of Trent held that works before justifying grace cannot merit grace, but after justifying grace we can merit final justification (i.e., eternal life) through cooperating with grace. The Protestant Reformation challenged this whole legalistic schema by contending that no Christian can merit God's favor.[30]

What Bloesch calls a "legalistic schema" the Reformers saw as an entire *system* of religion. The merit-grace issue was not a pedantic quarrel among technical theologians; it was a struggle between opposing systems. Bloesch echoes the sentiments expressed by Calvin: "In short, the name of Christ excludes all merit, and everything which men have of themselves; for when he says that we are chosen in Christ, it follows that in ourselves we are unworthy."[31]

Rome's view of merit and grace contains an unresolved paradox. On the one hand Rome insists on speaking of merit, while on the other she insists that this merit is rooted in grace. The Germans expressed this paradox by coining the term *Gnadenlohn*, "gracious merit."

This idea has its roots in the teaching of St. Augustine. He recognized that the New Testament speaks of "rewards" for believers in heaven. These rewards are distributed "according to" our works. But what does "according to" mean? Does it mean that our works deserve or merit a reward, either condignly or congruously? Or does it mean something else?

Augustine spoke of "God's crowning his own gifts." The Reformers understood this to mean that, though God distributes rewards *according to* our works, it remains a gracious distribution and is based on no merit inhering in them. James Buchanan says, ". . . Augustine, in common with all the Latin Fathers, used the term *merits,* not to denote legal, or moral desert, properly so called, but to signify, either simply a means of obtaining some blessing, or, at the most, an action that is rewardable, not 'of debt, but of grace.'"[32]

Augustine insisted that even the best works of sinners are still tainted by sin and are therefore but "splendid vices." Splendid vices are not morally equivalent to true virtues, and as such they can make no moral or legal claim on God for reward. Even in a state of grace, we are unprofitable servants.

The Rejection of Human Merit

In common language *merit* is usually understood in distinction from grace. The two are polar opposites. To conjoin them paradoxically in certain contexts into a concept of "gracious merit" sounds like an oxymoron. The New Testament sharply distinguishes between grace and debt. The Reformers made every effort to keep this distinction clean.

Be that as it may, Rome has labored to show that merit is rooted or grounded in grace. The new *Catechism of the Catholic Church* says:

> With regard to God, there is no strict right to any merit on the part of man. . . . The merit of man before God in the Christian life arises from the fact that *God has freely chosen to associate man with the work of his grace.* The fatherly action of God is first on his own initiative, and then follows man's free acting through his collaboration, so that the merit of good works is to be attributed in the first place to the grace of God, then to the faithful. Man's merit, moreover, itself is due to God, for his good actions proceed in Christ, from the predispositions and assistance given by the Holy Spirit.[33]

Human merit is real and effective. It is impossible, however, to have such merit except via grace. The merit of the believer rests on the prior and initiatory grace of Christ. Cooperation with that grace, however, yields real merit.

For Rome grace makes human merit possible. For the Reformers grace makes such merit impossible. If we do what we do by grace, then it is seriously misleading to speak of merit at all.

Rome and the Reformers agreed that the *ultimate* meritorious ground of our justification is found in the merit of Christ, but not the immediate grounds. We may call this the *objective ground* of our justification. But *how* is the objective merit of Christ appropriated by the sinner? The Reformers insisted that the merit of Christ and the benefits of his saving work are applied freely to the sinner by faith alone. Rome has the sinner doing necessary works of satisfaction by which he gains congruous merit in order to be justified by Christ. In a not-so-subtle manner this means that the sinner must merit the merit of Christ. Salvation is accomplished through the merit of Christ and on the merit of the believer.

Again, Rome declares that this gracious merit becomes true human merit: "Filial adoption, in making us partakers by grace in the divine nature, can bestow *true merit* on us as a result of God's gratuitous justice.... The merits of our good works are gifts of the divine goodness. . . . 'Our merits are God's gifts.'"[34]

Here the *Catechism* appeals to Trent, specifically to chapter 16 of the sixth session.

Thomas Aquinas explained "gracious merit" as follows:

> A man's meritorious work may be considered in two ways; in so far as it proceeds from his own free will, and in so far as it proceeds from the grace of the Holy Spirit. There cannot be condignity if a meritorious work is considered as it is in its own substance, and as the outcome of a man's own free will, since there is then extreme inequality. There is, however, congruity, since there is a certain relative equality. For it seems congruous that if a man works according to his own power, God should reward him according to the excellence of his power. But if we are speaking of a meritorious work as proceeding from the grace of the Holy Spirit, it merits eternal life condignly.[35]

Again we see the notion of "gracious merit" that is nevertheless real merit. The Catholic tradition seeks to distance itself from any crass sense of self-righteousness based on mere human merit. Hans Küng insists that Christ himself sharply denounced the pharisaical morality of merit: "*Christus hat scharf gegen die pharisäische Verdienstmoral gesprochen.*"[36]

The Reformers rejected both the merit concept of the Pharisees and the merit concept of Rome. Luther said:

> These arguments of the Scholastics about the merit of congruence and of worthiness (*de merito congrui et condigni*) are nothing but vain figments and dreamy speculations of idle folk about worthless stuff. Yet they form the foundation of the papacy, and on them it rests to this very day. For this is what every monk imagines: By observing the sacred rules of my order I can earn the grace of congruence, but by the works I do after I have received this grace I can accumulate a merit so great that it will not only be enough to bring me to eternal life but enough to sell and give it to others.[37]

Luther goes on to say:

> There is no such thing as merit; but all who are justified are justi-
> fied for nothing (*gratis*), and this is credited to no one but to the
> grace of God. . . . For Christ alone it is proper to help and save oth-
> ers with His merits and works. The works of others are of benefit
> to no one, not to themselves either; for the statement stands: "The
> just shall live by faith" (Rom. 1:17). For faith grounds us on the
> works of Christ, without our own works, and transfers us from the
> exile of our sins into the kingdom of His righteousness. This is
> faith; this [is] the Gospel; this is Christ.[38]

In less strident terms Calvin affirmed the same sentiment:
"First, I must premise with regard to the term *Merit*, that he, whoever he was, that first applied it to human works, viewed in reference to the divine tribunal, consulted very ill for the purity of
the faith. . . . what need was there to introduce the word *Merit*,
when the value of works might have been fully expressed by
another term, and without offence?"[39]

In summary, the Reformers strenuously objected to assigning
any merit to our justification save the merit of Christ alone. Again,
we see that the *sola gratia* of the Reformation was a true *sola*,
without mixture of any type of human merit. *Sola fide* meant that
justification is by faith alone because it is a justification by the
imputed merit of Christ alone.

We dream not of a faith
which is devoid of good works,
nor of a justification
which can exist without them: . . . .
while we acknowledge
that faith and works
are necessarily connected,
we, however, place justification
in faith, not in works. . . . .

John Calvin

Faith and Works

The debate over justification often suffers from a crass caricature by which the Reformed position is characterized as "justification by faith" and the Roman Catholic position is characterized as "justification by works." Popular sentiment tends to conclude that Rome is not concerned with faith and that the Reformers were not concerned about works.

As we have seen in the merit-grace debate, this characterization, stated in such simplistic terms, represents a false dilemma. We have already seen that Rome gives an important—indeed necessary—place to faith, and that the Reformers saw saving faith as necessarily, inevitably, and immediately yielding the fruit of works. Martin Luther insisted that the faith that justifies is a *fides viva*, a vital and living faith that yields the fruit of works. Justification is by faith alone, but not by a faith that is alone. Saving faith is not a "lonely" faith, having no works following as a companion.

John Gerstner uses two formulas, depicted in figure 8.1, to distinguish between the two views. The three terms *faith*, *works*, and

Fig. 8.1
Faith and Works

Roman Catholic View	Faith + Works———→Justification
Reformation View	Faith———→Justification + Works

justification are present in both formulas. The difference in the *order* of these terms in the two equations, however, points to the radical difference between the two positions. In the Roman formula works are a necessary precondition *for* justification. In the Reformed view works are a necessary fruit *of* justification.

Works and Justification

A recurring complaint among Protestant theologians is that Trent's canons and decrees on justification are at times fuzzy. They frequently miss the mark and reveal serious misunderstanding of the Reformers' views. Canon 24, however, does not suffer in this way. Here Rome is precise in condemning the Reformed view: "If anyone says that the justice received is not preserved and also not increased before God through good works, but that those works are merely the fruits and signs of justification obtained, but not the cause of its increase, let him be anathema."[1]

John Calvin said of canon 24: "That God visits the good works of the godly with reward, and to [the] former adds new and ampler grace, we deny not. But whoever asserts that works have the effect of increasing justification, understands neither . . . the meaning of justification nor its cause. That we are regarded as righteous when we are accepted by God, has already been proved. From this acceptance, too, works derive whatever grace they had."[2]

Calvin protests that Trent's canon 24 demonstrates that Rome understands neither the nature of the biblical concept of justification nor its cause. Far from a simple misunderstanding, the two sides were locked in an irreconcilable conflict between exclusive views of both the nature and the cause of justification.

If there is a point to quibble with Rome about in canon 24, this is it. Rome speaks of works being considered (presumably by the Reformers) as being "*merely* the fruits and signs of justification." The Reformers did consider works to be fruits and signs of justification, but they did not consider this a small or insignificant thing, as might be suggested by the word *merely*.

Likewise canon 32 of Trent provoked a strong protest from Calvin and the Reformers with respect to the role of works in justification: "If anyone says that the good works of the one justified are in such manner the gifts of God that they are not also the good merits of him justified; or that the one justified by the good works that he performs by the grace of God and the merit of Jesus Christ, whose living member he is, does not truly merit an increase of grace, eternal life, and in case he dies in grace, the attainment of eternal life itself and also an increase of glory, let him be anathema."[3]

If we extend Gerstner's formula to incorporate the elements of this canon, it would look something like figure 8.2. Again, this formula indicates that the believer's good works and merit, though rooted in the grace of God and the merit of Christ, are nevertheless the necessary preconditions for one's justification and the cause of it.

Calvin responded to canon 32 by saying:

By what right or in what sense the Good Works which the Spirit of Christ performs in us are called ours, Augustine briefly teaches when he draws an analogy from the Lord's Prayer: saying, that the bread which we there ask is called "ours" on no other ground than simply that it is given to us. Accordingly, as the same writer elsewhere teaches, no man will embrace the gifts of Christ till he has forgotten his own merits. He sometimes gives the reason: because, what is called merit is nought else but the free gift of God.[4]

For the Reformers the good works that flow out of justification are not good enough to meet the perfect demands of the law of God. Our best works remain tainted or soiled by the vestigial remnants of sin. Our hearts are never perfectly pure, and this impurity adds dross to the "gold" of our virtues. Our virtues remain, as

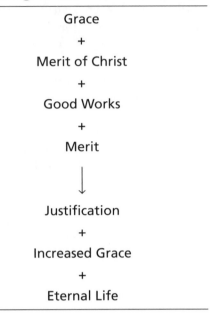

Fig. 8.2
**Grace and Merit
According to the Council of Trent**

Grace

+

Merit of Christ

+

Good Works

+

Merit

↓

Justification

+

Increased Grace

+

Eternal Life

Augustine declared, splendid vices. Luther said this about our good works:

> . . . because of the restraining influence of our native corruption we do not even do our good works with a motive and in a purity that measure up to the requirements of the Law, seeing that we do not do them with all our might but only in the power of the Spirit that fights against the power of the flesh. This is why we sin even when we do good if God, through Christ, did not cover up this imperfection of ours but imputed it to us. So the sin of the good work becomes venial through the mercy of God. Because we believe and sigh over the imperfection which has been assumed in Christ, God does not impute the sin to us.
> Therefore the man is excessively stupid who fancies that he must be regarded just because of his works although, when they are submitted to the judgment of God, they are sins and are found to be such.[5]

This sentiment, echoed by other Reformers, came under sharp attack at Trent. Canon 25 declares: "If anyone says that in every good work the just man sins at least venially, or, what is more intolerable, mortally, and hence merits eternal punishment, and that he is not damned for this reason only, because God does not impute these works unto damnation, let him be anathema."[6]

Here the anathema of Rome hangs heavy over the heads of the Reformers. This blast hit its intended target squarely. Calvin responded: "In the judgment of God nothing is genuine and good, save what flows from perfect love to Him. If the heart of man is never reformed so far in this life, as not to labour under many defects, and to be distracted by various passions, and often tickled by worldly allurements, works must of necessity carry some taint along with them. There is no work, therefore, which is not sin, unless it acquires a value in consequence of a gratuitous estimate."[7]

Calvin rejected the Roman Catholic distinction between mortal and venial sin. On the one hand all sins of believers are mortal (in the sense that all sin *deserves* death). On the other hand no sin is mortal to the believer in the sense that it destroys the grace of justification.

Though they considered the works that flow out of justification tainted by sin, the Reformers nevertheless spoke of them as "good works," in the sense that they correspond to some degree to the commands of Christ. Calvin says:

> We dream not of a faith which is devoid of good works, nor of a justification which can exist without them: the only difference is, that while we acknowledge that faith and works are necessarily connected, we, however, place justification in faith, not in works. . . . Because by faith we apprehend the righteousness of Christ, which alone reconciles us to God. This faith, however, you cannot apprehend without at the same time apprehending sanctification. . . . Christ, therefore, justifies no man without also sanctifying him.[8]

Calvin insists on a real *connection* between faith and works and between justification and sanctification. These may and must be distinguished from one another, but they must not be separated. The connection between them is a necessary one. God has joined them together lest any man rend them asunder. Faith without works is a mere dream of fancy. It is a moral and spiritual impossibility. Yet they must be distinguished clearly in order to grasp the biblical notion of justification by faith. Calvin, like Paul, places justification *in* faith, not in works, precisely because it is the work of Christ, not our own, that justifies us.

Rome also links justification and sanctification, but in reverse order. For Rome justification rests on sanctification; for the Reformers, sanctification flows out of, by necessary connection, justification. Calvin concludes: "But you cannot possess him without being made a partaker of his sanctification: for Christ cannot be divided. Since the Lord, therefore, does not grant us the enjoyment of these blessings without bestowing himself, he bestows both at once, but never the one without the other. Thus it appears how true it is that we are justified not without, and yet not by works, since in the participation of Christ, by which we are justified, is contained not less sanctification than justification."[9]

Justification by Faith *Alone*

In its clear rejection of *sola fide*, the Roman Catholic Church objected to the term *sola*. Catholic theologians granted that justification is by faith, but not that it is by faith alone. On the one hand they argued that the word *alone* is absent from the New Testament (particularly Paul's epistles) when it speaks of justification. On the other hand they pointed to the Epistle of James, where the doctrine of justification by faith *alone* appears to be specifically repudiated. James 2:17 and 20 is cited by Trent in chapter 7 of the sixth session. Chapter 10 then cites James 2:24, "Do you see that by works a man is justified, and not by faith only."[10]

With respect to the first objection (the absence of the word *alone* in the text of Scripture), Calvin replied: "The reader now perceives with what fairness the Sophists of the present day cavil at our doctrine, when we say that a man is justified by faith alone (Rom. 4:2). They dare not deny that 'he is justified by faith,' seeing Scripture so often declares it; but as the word *alone* is nowhere expressly used, they will not tolerate its being added."[11]

Calvin concedes that the word *alone* does not appear in the text of Paul's exposition of justification. He insists, however, that the *concept* is plainly there:

> What answer, then, will they give to the words of Paul, when he contends that righteousness is not of faith unless it be gratuitous? How can it be gratuitous, and yet by works? . . . The Law, therefore, has no part in it, and their objection to the exclusive word *alone* is not only unfounded, but is obviously absurd. Does he not plainly enough attribute everything to faith alone when he disconnects it with works? What, I would ask, is meant by the expressions, "The righteousness of God without the law is manifest"; "Being justified freely by his grace"; "Justified by faith without the deeds of the Law"? (Rom. 3:21, 24, 28).[12]

Luther also responded to the criticism that the word *alone* does not appear in Romans:

> Note, then, whether Paul does not assert more vehemently that faith alone justifies than I do, although he does not use the word *alone* (*sola*), which I have used. For he who says: Works do not justify, but faith justifies, certainly affirms more strongly that faith justifies than does he who says: Faith alone justifies. . . . It is ridiculous enough to argue in this sophistical manner: Faith alone justifies; therefore the Holy Spirit does not justify. Or: The Spirit justifies; therefore not faith alone. For this is not what the dispute is about at this place. Rather the question is only about the relation of faith and works, whether anything is to be ascribed to works in justification. Since the apostle does not ascribe anything to them, he without a doubt ascribes all to faith alone.[13]

More formidable is the Catholic appeal to the Epistle of James and the statement, "Do you see that by works a man is justified, and not by faith only." This bold statement seems, at least on the surface, to contradict flatly the Reformation view of *sola fide*. The problem is exacerbated by James's earlier statement regarding

Abraham: "Was not Abraham our father justified by works, in that he offered up Isaac his son on the altar?" (2:21).

The apparent conflict between Paul and James on the issue of faith and works has provoked a multitude of theories and attempts at harmonization. G. C. Berkouwer summarizes the options more frequently offered by scholars:

> 1. James was consciously polemicizing against the teaching of Paul (which assumes that Paul's Epistle to the Romans was written before the Epistle of James).
>
> 2. James polemicized, not against Paul, but against an antinomian misconception of Paul's witness to justification by faith.
>
> 3. Paul's letter to the Romans and the Epistle of James have a different problem in view and are not struggling with each other at all.[14]

We could add a fourth option: James wrote his epistle before Paul wrote Romans, and Paul sought to correct James in his epistle to the Romans.

This last option (as well as option 1) raises some serious problems. First, it presupposes a disunity and disharmony in Scripture itself, a position rejected by both classical Roman Catholicism and classical Reformation thought, though allowed by advocates of modern critical theories of Scripture.

Second, neither Paul nor James names or refers to the other in any way in their epistles. This is an argument from silence, but it would be strange for such a sharp difference in the apostolic church not to be explicitly stated. Paul did not hesitate to name Peter in the Epistle to the Galatians, mentioning their conflict over the gospel.

And third, if either option 1 or 4 is correct, any blame for the furious debate of the Reformation should be laid at the feet, not of the Reformers or the Roman Catholic Church, but of the Apostles themselves.

Most commentators favor option 2 or 3, or a combination of the two. That James has little time for antinomianism is plain from the content and tone of his entire epistle. That he is treating a different subject from Paul should also be clear from a careful reading of both epistles.

James does say, however, that a man is justified by works and not by faith only. It is even more burdensome that both Paul and James appeal to the patriarch Abraham to prove their cases. Paul argues that Abraham was justified when he believed God in Genesis 15. James argues that Abraham was justified when he offered Isaac on the altar in Genesis 22. Both appeal to Abraham, but for different reasons and at different times in Abraham's life. They also use the same Greek words for *faith* and *justify*. The question remains, Are they speaking of the same thing when using these terms?

Calvin answers no: "... it will be easy to see where the error of our opponents lies. They fall into a double paralogism, the one in the term *faith*, the other in the term *justifying*. The Apostle, in giving the name of *faith* to an empty opinion altogether differing from true faith, makes a concession which derogates in no respect from his case."[15]

Calvin then speaks of the other paralogism with respect to the word *justify*: "If you would make James consistent with the other Scriptures and with himself, you must give the word *justify*, as used by him, a different meaning from what it has with Paul."[16]

In theological discourse words are often used with subtle differences of meaning and nuance. When apparent conflicts arise, it is prudent, for clarity's sake, to ask, What concerns are being expressed by the different writers? What problems are they trying to solve?

Different Concerns

Clearly Paul and James are not occupied with identical concerns. Neither are they addressing the same problem. Paul is concerned with the theological issue of how a sinner may be considered righteous before the tribunal of God. He is expounding the gospel of justification.

James's concern is somewhat different. He specifies the question he is answering: "What good is it, my brothers, if someone says that he professes faith but does not have works? Can his faith save him?" (2:14).

James is giving no full-orbed treatment of the doctrine of justification. Gerhard Kittel's *Theological Dictionary of the New Testament* indicates: "Characteristic of James' treatment of the subject is his campaign against a dead orthodoxy which speaks of faith but does not take works seriously."[17]

James makes it clear that a mere *profession* of faith does not result in salvation. There is no profit in a profession of faith that yields no works. He is answering the question, What kind of faith saves? He specifically asks, Can his (this kind of) faith save him? His answer is a resounding no. A faith devoid of works is not a saving faith. At this point there is no disagreement with Paul or with the Reformers. All insist that the faith that justifies is one that necessarily manifests itself in works. Here Berkouwer's option 2 is in view: the Epistle of James is a polemic against any form of antinomianism that will boast of justification by a faith without works.

James declares in verse 17: "Thus also faith by itself, if it does not have works, is dead" (NKJV). A mere profession of faith unaccompanied by works is not only unprofitable but "dead." How is the word *dead* used here? Some have argued that it refers to someone who once had faith but whose faith subsequently perished. James uses the term *dead* three times in this discussion (2:14–26), concluding with the analogy of a dead body: "For as the body without the spirit is dead, so faith without works is dead also" (2:26 NKJV).

Zane Hodges commented on this:

> If I were walking down the street one day and encountered a dead body, I could easily conclude two things. First, I could conclude that the body no longer contained its life-giving spirit, and second, that this body had once actually been alive. One thing I would most certainly not conclude. I would not conclude that the body had never been alive at all.

Yet, in one of the strangest distortions of Scripture that has ever occurred, many theologians and Bible interpreters have decided that a "dead faith" must necessarily have always been dead.[18]

Elsewhere Hodges wrote: "Not only is there no commonly accepted interpretation of James 2:14–26 in post-Reformation Protestantism, but indeed all of the major ways of reading this text are wrong. *And not simply wrong, but seriously so.* So incorrect are these views, that if James himself had heard them, he would have been both astonished and appalled!"[19]

D. A. Carson, astonished by Hodges's interpretation of James, wrote: ". . . to the best of my knowledge not one significant interpreter of Scripture in the entire history of the church has held to Hodges's interpretation of the passages he treats. This does not necessarily mean Hodges is wrong; but it certainly means he is probably wrong. . . ."[20]

For the moment we will leave Hodges contemplating the corpse-in-the-street and look at more conventional understandings of James. Alexander Ross argued that James used *dead* to refer to a condition of barrenness. *Dead* does not refer to a faith that was once alive or was stillborn. Ross remarked: "*Barren* . . . is probably the true reading, not 'dead.' This word means, literally, *without work*, producing nothing of any importance. It is translated 'idle' in Mt. 20:3 and 6, in 1 Tim. 5:13, in Titus 1:2. . . . It occurs again in 2 Pet. 1:8. . . ."[21]

In 2:18 James continues his argument: "But someone will say, 'You have faith, and I have works.' Show me your faith without your works, and I will show you my faith by my works" (NKJV). Here James speaks of the demonstration or manifestation of faith by works. The believer shows true faith at the human level by visible actions. Scripture reminds us that we "know" the believer by his fruit, but also that we can see only outward appearances. God has the ability to read the heart. It is not necessary for God to observe outward actions to know if true faith is present in the heart. Our works "justify" our claim to faith in the eyes of human beholders. Such "justification" or vindication is not necessary for God.

Perhaps this helps account for the different circumstances in Abraham's life to which Paul and James appeal. James says, "Was not Abraham our father justified by works when he offered Isaac his son on the altar?" (2:21 NKJV).

The question remains, Before whom was Abraham justified and in what sense was Abraham justified? If we say Abraham was justified before God in the theological sense of *justify*, then we are in serious conflict with Paul. In Romans 4 Paul labors the point that Abraham was not justified by works:

> What then shall we say that Abraham our father has found according to the flesh? For if Abraham was justified by works, he has *something of which* to boast, but not before God. For what does the Scripture say? "Abraham believed God, and it was accounted to him for righteousness." Now to him who works, the wages are not counted as grace but as debt. But to him who does not work but believes on Him who justifies the ungodly, his faith is accounted for righteousness. . . . (Rom. 4:1–5 NKJV).

Paul declares that Abraham was justified *before* he performed works. He was justified as soon as he had faith (in Gen. 15). Abraham is reckoned or counted as righteous (a forensic declaration) before and without a view to his works.

Later Abraham demonstrated his faith by his works of obedience. In this sense we are reminded of Jesus' figurative use of *justify*: "Wisdom is justified by her children." Jesus is obviously not saying that wisdom is reconciled to God by having babies. He is saying that true wisdom is made manifest, or demonstrated to be true wisdom, from the fruit it yields.

Perhaps this is close to what James means when he speaks of Abraham as "justified" by his works. James says this in the context of showing or demonstrating true faith by the fruit of works. He is clearly aware that Abraham had already been reckoned righteous by God (Gen. 15). James alludes to this when he says: "Do you see that faith was working together with his works, and by works faith was made perfect? And the Scripture was fulfilled which says, 'Abraham believed God, and it was accounted to him for righteousness'" (James 2:22–23 NKJV).

James nowhere says that the *ground* of Abraham's justification before God was his works. He nowhere assigns any merit to Abraham's works. The *ground* of justification, which is at the heart of Paul's concern in Romans, is not the subject James is discussing. He is stressing the necessary connection between faith and works as integral to saving faith.

Again Calvin comments:

> If it is absurd to say that the effect was prior to its cause, either Moses falsely declares in that passage that Abraham's faith was imputed for righteousness, or Abraham, by his obedience in offering up Isaac, did not merit righteousness. Before the existence of Ishmael, who was a grown youth at the birth of Isaac, Abraham was justified by his faith. How then can we say that he obtained justification by an obedience which followed long after? Wherefore, either James erroneously inverts the proper order (this it were impious to suppose), or he meant not to say that he was justified, as if he deserved to be deemed just. What then? It appears certain that he is speaking of the manifestation, not of the imputation of righteousness, as if he had said, Those who are justified by true faith prove their justification by obedience and good works, not by a bare and imaginary semblance of faith. In one word, he is not discussing the mode of justification, but requiring that the justification of believers shall be operative.[22]

James, far from denying *sola fide,* is showing that the faith that justifies is not a faith that is alone. His treatment does not vitiate either Paul's or the Reformers' doctrine, though indeed it deals a fatal blow to all forms of antinomianism.

In Romans Paul declares: "Where *is* boasting then? It is excluded. By what law? Of works? No, but by the law of faith. Therefore we conclude that a man is justified by faith apart from the deeds of the law" (Rom. 3:27–28 NKJV).

The word *therefore* signifies that an apostolic conclusion is about to follow. Paul concludes unambiguously—that justification is by faith apart from the deeds of the law.

Charles Hodge says of this: "If by faith, it is not of works; and if not of works, there can be no room for boasting, for boasting is the assertion of personal merit. From the nature of the case, if justification is by faith, it must be by faith alone. Luther's version, therefore, '*allein durch den glauben,*' is fully justified by the context."[23]

Hodge also notes that, though modern Roman Catholics protest Luther's insertion of the word *allein,* Catholic translators before Luther had done the same: "So in the Nuremberg Bible (1483), '*Nur durch den glauben.*' And the Italian Bibles of Geneva (1476) and of Venice (1538), '*per sola fede.*'"[24]

Christ as Savior and Lord

Though historic Evangelicalism has been unified and monolithic in its understanding of *sola fide* and of the connection between faith and works, that unity was ruptured in our day by a major controversy that erupted within the household of dispensationalism. The chief opponents in this rift were John MacArthur on one side and Zane Hodges and Charles Ryrie on the other.

Advocates of "Lordship salvation" argue that saving faith involves embracing Christ as both Savior and Lord and that true faith inevitably, necessarily, and immediately begins to display the fruit of obedience. That is, the process of sanctification by which we are conformed to the image of Christ begins certainly and immediately upon our justification. This process of sanctification is neither perfect in this life nor is it in any way the *ground* of our justification. This ground remains exclusively the righteousness of Christ imputed to us by faith alone. But the justified person is manifestly a *changed* person who is regenerated and indwelt by the Holy Spirit. He acknowledges, embraces, and to some degree submits to Christ as Lord.

The non-Lordship camp acknowledges that every Christian should embrace the Lordship of Christ and manifest the fruit of faith. The fruit of faith, however, has no necessary connection to justification. It is possible to be a "carnal Christian": saving faith may be present without any subsequent manifestation of it through works. It is possible, though not desirable, for a person to receive Jesus as Savior without in any way embracing him as Lord. Neither repentance nor submission to Christ's Lordship is a necessary element of saving faith. To make it necessary is legalism and a tacit denial of the free grace of the gospel. It is no accident that Zane Hodges's book on the subject is entitled *Absolutely Free!* Hodges and Ryrie are convinced they are defending the purity of the gospel of grace. MacArthur and the Lordship camp are convinced they are defending the biblical gospel from antinomianism.

This book is not the place for an in-depth analysis or evaluation of this controversy. I mention it in passing merely to note that the doctrine of justification remains in dispute in our time, not only between historic Roman Catholicism and Reformed theology, but also among professing Evangelicals.

Ryrie makes it clear that the fruit of works will occur inevitably in the life of every Christian: "Every Christian will bear spiritual fruit. Somewhere, sometime, somehow. Otherwise that person is not a believer. Every born-again individual will be fruitful. Not to be fruitful is to be faithless, without faith, and therefore without salvation."[25]

The point in dispute here is not the inevitability of spiritual fruit, but *when* it will appear. The Reformed position argues that fruit begins immediately, because a justified person is a regenerate person and a regenerate person is a changed person. He is also a repentant person whose "change of mind" is integral to saving faith.

Neither Ryrie nor Hodges wants to see repentance or fruit as *requirements* of salvation. Hodges says: "If we keep this fact firmly in mind, we will never make the mistake of thinking that repentance is a condition for eternal salvation."[26]

Hodges appeals to Calvin's rejection of the identification of repentance and faith, citing Calvin's comment: "For to include faith in repentance, is repugnant to what Paul says in Acts [20:21] ... where he mentions faith and repentance, as two things totally distinct."[27]

Calvin indeed *distinguishes* between faith and repentance and argues strenuously that faith is not produced by repentance. Yet Calvin will not separate or disconnect repentance from faith.

Calvin says: "That repentance not only always follows faith, but is produced by it, ought to be without controversy. . . . It is certain that no man can embrace the grace of the Gospel without betaking himself from the errors of his former life into the right path and making it his whole study to practise repentance."[28]

Earlier Calvin says: "The sum of the Gospel is, not without good reason, made to consist in repentance and forgiveness of sins; and, therefore, where these two heads are omitted, any discussion concerning faith will be meagre and defective, and indeed almost useless."[29]

That Calvin was jealous to distinguish faith and repentance without separating them is made crystal clear when he writes: "Can true repentance exist without faith? By no means. But although they cannot be separated, they ought to be distinguished. As there is no faith without hope, and yet faith and hope are different, so repentance and faith, though constantly linked together, are only to be united, not confounded. I am not unaware that under the term *repentance* is comprehended the whole work of turning to God, of which not the least important part is faith. . . ."[30] Calvin will not allow for a repentance without faith. Neither will he allow for a faith without repentance.

Hodges insists that repentance is necessary for fellowship with God, but not for salvation:

> It is an extremely serious matter when the biblical distinction between faith and repentance is collapsed and when repentance is thus made a condition for eternal life. For under this perception of things the New Testament doctrine of faith is radically rewritten and held hostage to the demand for repentance. . . . though genuine repentance *may* precede salvation. . . , it *need not* do so. And because it is not essential to the saving transaction as such, it is in no sense a condition for that transaction. But the fact still remains that God demands repentance from all and He conditions their *fellowship with Him* on that.[31]

Hodges acknowledges that God *requires* repentance as a condition for fellowship with him, yet insists that God does not *require* it for eternal salvation. Does this mean that the impenitent can and will inherit eternal life? Does it mean a believer can be justified and saved without having fellowship with God? I can hardly believe Hodges means what he says. This is antinomianism with a vengeance.

To be sure, Calvin vigorously opposed the sacrament of penance as a requirement or necessary condition of salvation. This is not to say that he opposed repentance as a requirement for salvation.

But what is meant by *requirement* or *condition*? Both Ryrie and Hodges are deeply concerned that repentance not be the *ground* of our justification. They fear this would obscure the true ground, the righteousness of Christ, and make repentance a *work* that destroys *sola fide*.

Calvin treats repentance in a manner similar to works. Works are not the ground of our justification or our salvation, but there will be no salvation without them. As one cannot have true faith without it yielding works, so one cannot have true faith without simultaneously having repentance. In that sense repentance is necessary for salvation. If there is no repentance, there is not only no fellowship with God but also no salvation, precisely because the lack of repentance proves that there is no genuine faith.

Let it therefore remain settled . . .
that we are justified
in no other way than by faith,
or, which comes to the same thing,
that we are justified by faith alone.

John Calvin

No Other Gospel

The tone of the Reformation debate was clearly polemical. Each side was strident and at times vehement in its denunciations of the other. They called each other scurrilous names, and the battle escalated to the level of blood. There were inquisition, persecution, heresy trials, torture, and executions. All of this seems almost surrealistic from the vantage point of the twentieth century.

As we approach the twenty-first century, we live in a world and a culture that has had a belly full of conflict. Our century has been marked by two world wars, massive slaughters in Germany, the former Soviet Union, Africa, and Southeast Asia. Religious conflict has ripped nations apart, with terrorism emerging as an art form. In America we have endured racial conflict, the battle of the sexes, fierce political estrangement, the abortion struggle, and a host of other points of serious division. Add to these things the nuclear Sword of Damocles that hangs over all our heads, and it is no surprise that we shrink from further conflict.

A new climate has emerged. It rests on the precarious foundation of philosophical relativism and pluralism. This foundation was not created out of a passion for truth or the quest for a sound epistemology. It was designed by architects who seek to create a world or national community where people of differing political, moral, philosophical, and religious views can live together in harmony and peace. If truth can be viewed as relative or pluralistic, then it follows resistlessly that no one can justly claim any final or exclusive truth. The only ultimate truth becomes the assertion that there is no ultimate truth. This is manifestly a self-referential absurdity. If there is no ultimate truth, then the assertion "There is no ultimate truth" is no more true or false than the assertion "There is ultimate truth."

For relativism or pluralism to work, for it to achieve its goal of establishing peace and harmony, it must have as its core principle that of *toleration*. This principle itself, however, cannot be absolute, because the law of toleration intolerantly forbids intolerance.

I live in a country, the United States, that prides itself on its long heritage of religious toleration. People fled to these shores to avoid persecution for their religious convictions. We have a national pact, a solemn agreement, to tolerate the free exercise of religion. No one religious faith or sect is "established" as a state church.

That all religions are tolerated, however, does not mean that all religions are equally valid, or that each religion must tolerate all theological views. Each religion has its own standards for membership. Violations of those standards may and often do involve exclusion from membership. Churches still practice the discipline of excommunication, and though increasingly rare they still have trials or tribunals over questions of heresy. But the civil government does not intrude (for the most part) in such cases. The state does not burn people at the stake for heresy.

The Reality of Heresy

This does not mean that there is no longer any such thing as heresy. Perhaps the climate has become one in which "none dare call it heresy." But heresy still exists as a problem, and churches still, as the church has always had to do, must address problems of theological error and heresy.

No theological issue in all of church history has produced such a volatile and divisive situation as that of justification by faith alone. Perhaps some would like to erase the sixteenth century from the record of history, but in reality it is ineradicable. The debate happened, and its consequences accrue to this day.

We do not live in the sixteenth century. That is the past. The problems we face in our day are different from those they faced then. We have learned to some degree to live without bloodshed over theological issues. A sanguine view of this is that we have matured and become more sanctified than our forbears who fought the battle in the sixteenth century. A less sanguine view is that there has been not evolution but devolution, not progress but regress.

If we are more tolerant because we have become more loving toward God and people, then the more sanguine view is in order. If we are more tolerant because we have become more ignorant of the gospel or more lax in its defense, then the less sanguine view is in order.

One thing is certain. Though the historical context and even the issues themselves may change from century to century, the gospel itself cannot change. We may seek to change it. We may seek to revise it. We may alter its content, but then it is no longer the gospel.

Both sides in the fierce conflict of the sixteenth century were convinced that they were contending for the gospel. It is possible that both sides erred in their understanding of the gospel's essence. It is also possible that one side had it essentially correct and the other side did not. It is impossible that both sides were right. Both could have had *valid concerns,* but their *conclusions* cannot both be right because these were and are mutually exclusive. The only way to avoid that conclusion realistically is to embrace epistemological relativism, which is suicidal to both sides in particular and to Christianity in general.

Though we may cringe at times at the intemperance and strident hostility expressed by both sides during the Reformation, we must at least recognize that both sides understood what was at stake. Let modern revisionists declare that it was a tempest in a teapot. Certainly the parties involved at the time did not regard it as such. Both Rome and the Reformers believed that the stakes were high, that the conflict involved a question of apostasy.

Most theologians agree that not all errors of doctrine warrant the charge of apostasy. The consensus is that only errors regarding essentials of Christianity warrant this charge. Not everyone agrees on what is essential. There are bodies claiming to be Christian, such as the Mormon "church" and Jehovah's Witnesses, that believe you can be a Christian without affirming the deity of Christ. Indeed, they regard this affirmation as an error. They consider the doctrine of Christ's deity to be heresy.

Historic Roman Catholicism and Protestantism, at least until the advent of nineteenth-century liberalism, have agreed that the deity of Christ is essential to Christianity. They agree on other essentials, such as the atonement and the resurrection of Christ. Modern liberalism has challenged this consensus, but this challenge is a relatively recent development.

Both historic Roman Catholicism and Reformation confessions affirm a large body of *catholic* doctrine, affirming, for example, the so-called ecumenical creeds. The questions that remain are these:

1. Is *sola fide* essential to the gospel?
2. Is the gospel essential to Christianity and to salvation?
3. Is the denial of the gospel an act of apostasy?

In the sixteenth century both Rome and the Reformers gave the same answer to questions 2 and 3. Both sides agreed that the gospel is essential to Christianity and that the denial of the gospel is an act of apostasy, even if the parties who deny it hold to all other essentials of Christianity.

The debate then and the debate now focus on question 1: Is *sola fide* essential to the gospel? The Reformers answered this question with a categorical affirmative. Rome answered with a categorical negative. Rome not only denied that *sola fide* is essential to the gospel, she denied it altogether. She declared it a pernicious heresy and put her emphatic and unambiguous anathema on it.

It is to Rome's credit, in my opinion, that she placed her anathema on what she believed to be a false and heretical gospel. If *sola fide* is a distortion of the biblical gospel, surely it deserves such anathema. If the Reformers were preaching and teaching a false gospel, then they were apostate and deserved the labels put on them by Vatican I: "schismatics and heretics."

Surely the Catholic Church of the sixteenth century did not consciously and intentionally condemn the gospel. I trust that the churchmen of Rome condemned what they believed was heresy. If in fact *sola fide* is a heresy, then Rome did the right thing. If, on the other hand, *sola fide* is the very essence of the gospel, then in her misguided zeal Rome condemned the gospel. If the true gospel is condemned after careful deliberation, then that condemnation, intentional or not, is an act of apostasy.

It may seem strange to speak of "unintentional" apostasy. When God judges our actions, surely he considers our intentions along with our actions. To condemn the gospel intentionally is obviously more heinous than to do so unintentionally. But unintentional heresy is still heresy, as both sides agreed.

Rome's moral theology distinguishes between sins done knowingly and those done in ignorance. Catholic theologians distinguish between vincible and invincible ignorance, a distinction that covers a multitude of sins. Ignorance that is invincible cannot be overcome. Ignorance that is vincible *can* and *should* be overcome. For example, if the Bible is hopelessly ambiguous about the essence of the gospel, then either side in the sixteenth century could appeal to invincible ignorance to ameliorate or cancel guilt. Yet both sides argued that the Bible is not ambiguous. Therefore neither side hesitated to call the other apostate. They agreed on at least one thing: one side taught heresy about an essential doctrine and that side was apostate.

This issue is not as sharply defined today. The fuzziness in our time has to do with the evangelical affirmation of *sola fide*. Many professed Evangelicals will unhesitatingly affirm *sola fide*. They believe *sola fide* is an important element of the gospel but is not *essential* to the gospel or salvation. S*ola fide* may be vital to the *bene esse* (well-being) of the church, but it is not vital to the *esse* (essence or being) of a true church.

For example, Evangelicals who signed *Evangelicals and Catholics Together* may believe that *sola fide* is the purest expression of the gospel but that it is not an essential Christian truth. Others may believe that it is essential but that Rome no longer denies it, escaping the state of apostasy.

The Essentials of the Faith

Is *sola fide* essential to the gospel, and is the gospel essential to salvation? What follows is a consideration of Paul's teaching on this in his Epistle to the Galatians.

First we must remember Paul's teaching regarding Christian behavior in the contexts of disputes. Paul tirelessly urges Christians to be gentle, kind, forbearing, and charitable with each other. By the same token he admonishes Christians not to be quarrelsome, back-biting, contentious, and divisive. For the apostle the disruption of Christian unity and of the peace of the church is no small thing. The spirit pervading his writing is one of a high level of tolerance in nonessential matters. When the apostle touches on matters he regards as essential to the Christian faith, however, he leaves no room for tolerance. Tolerating the intolerable was something Paul would not abide.

It is difficult to find in Paul's letters stronger rebuke or sharper admonishment than what he wrote to the Galatians. Here the apostle sees the gospel at stake, and he does not hesitate to speak in the strongest terms. After a brief salutation Paul moves quickly to address his deep concern about the Galatian situation: "I marvel that you are so quickly removing from him that called you in the grace of Christ unto a different Gospel" (1:6 ASV). Paul expresses apostolic amazement at the Galatians' rapid departure from the gospel. Herman Ridderbos says: "Right at the beginning the apostle raises the issue of the threatening apostasy of the churches of Galatia."[1]

Fig. 9.1
Paul's Letter to the Galatians

I marvel that you are so quickly removing
    from him that called you in the grace of Christ
    unto a different gospel;
      which is not another gospel:
only there are some that
    trouble you, and
    would pervert the gospel of Christ.

    But though we, or an angel from heaven,
    should preach unto you
      any gospel other than that
      which we preached unto you,
let him be anathema.
    As we have said before, so say I now again,
    If any man preacheth unto you
      any gospel other than that
      which you received,
let him be anathema.

For am I now seeking the favor of men, or of God?
Or am I striving to please men?
    If I were still pleasing men,
I should not be a servant of Christ.

For I make known to you, brethren,
    as touching the gospel
    which was preached by me,
    that it is not after man.
For neither did I receive it from man,
nor was I taught it,
but it came to me through revelation
    of Jesus Christ.

                    (Gal. 1:6–12)

Both John Calvin and Martin Luther note that Paul begins this section in a gentle manner. He expresses his shock at their moving away from the gospel. His words here are not filled with invective, because he is addressing the victims of the false teaching, not the perpetrators of it. Luther comments on the apostle's gentle and sweet words, designed to heal their wounds rather than stab them:

> We, too, should follow this example. We should show that toward those poor disciples who have been led astray we feel as parents feel toward their children, so that they may see our paternal zeal and maternal feelings toward them and may see that we seek their salvation. But when it comes to the devil and his servants, the originators of perversion and sectarianism, we should follow the example of the apostles. We should be impatient, proud, sharp, and bitter, despising and condemning their sham as sharply and harshly as we can. When a child has been bitten by a dog, the parents chase the dog but console and soothe the weeping child with the sweetest of words.[2]

It is interesting that in the 1535 edition of his *Commentary on Galatians* Luther's language is much sharper than in the 1519 edition. Our model for such disputes is neither Luther nor Calvin. Ultimately it is not even Paul. Paul reflects the ultimate model of Jesus himself, who was characteristically gentle and tender with the victims of false teaching but vehement in denouncing false teachers as serpents, dogs, and the like.

Though the apostle's rebuke is gentle, it is still a rebuke. Calvin notes:

> He charges the Galatians with defection, not only from his own teaching, but from Christ. For they could only keep to Christ by acknowledging that it is by His benefit that we are set free from the bondage of the law. . . . Thus they were removed from Christ, not in that they entirely rejected Christianity but because in such a corruption only a fictitious Christ was left to them. So today the Papists choose to have a half Christ and a mangled Christ and so none at all and are therefore removed from Christ.[3]

When Paul speaks of the Galatians having moved away from "him" who called you in the grace of Christ, Ridderbos takes this as a reference, not merely to Paul, but to God himself: "This *him* refers not merely to the proclaimer of the Gospel, Paul himself, but to God also. So much can be inferred from the term *called*, the technical term for the divine activity with the gospel. . . ."[4]

Paul expresses his amazement about three things: (1) that the Galatians have moved, (2) that they have moved away from the gospel of Christ, and (3) that they have moved so quickly.

The Present Crisis

Historic Evangelicalism was prepared to die for the gospel of justification by faith alone. Contemporary American Evangelicalism has moved away from the centrality of *sola fide* to the gospel. In J. I. Packer's 1994 article "Why I Signed It" in *Christianity Today*, he alludes to *sola fide* with the expression "small print." James Boice countered Packer's repeated use of the term *small print* in closed debate by declaring that *sola fide* is central and must be declared today in boldface type. What Packer in 1961 described as the "Atlas" of biblical doctrine that carries the world of the doctrine and life of the church on its shoulders, he now relegates to the "theory level" of doctrine. Atlas has shrugged, and the evangelical house totters on the brink of collapse.

In the controversy evoked by *Evangelicals and Catholics Together,* old alliances have crumbled and former allies have become opponents. Somebody moved. The movement seemed slight, but (as happens when a slight shift occurs in the earth's crust) an earthquake ensued. From Paul's vantage point, when the Galatians moved away from the purity of the gospel, the very foundation of the house of God shifted. The Psalmist had already asked what the righteous can do if the foundations are destroyed (11:3).

That is the crisis faced by the evangelical church as it enters the twenty-first century. The church is assailed on every side by the forces of modernity and an increasingly hostile secularism. We all feel the need to close ranks to protect the church from this onslaught. But if in closing ranks we shift the foundation of the faith, there will be no evangelical church left to protect.

In any age departures from biblical orthodoxy can come quickly and with little warning. When Paul refers to how "quickly" the Galatians have moved away from the gospel, the word *quickly* carries the implication of facility. That is, when something moves quickly, this movement is usually accomplished with ease. Reflecting on the church in Wittenberg in his day, Luther said:

> But some fanatic could stop this blessed progress of the Gospel in a hurry, and in one moment he could overturn everything that we have built up with the hard work of many years. This is what happened to Paul, the chosen instrument of Christ (Acts 9:15). With great toil and trouble he had gained the churches of Galatia; but in a short time after his departure the false apostles overthrew them, as this and all his other epistles testify. So weak and miserable is this present life, and so beset are we by the snares of Satan, that one fanatic can often destroy and completely undo in a short time what it took faithful ministers the hard labor of many years day and night to build up. We are learning this by bitter experience today, and yet there is nothing we can do about it.[5]

Luther's comment is revealing. It exposes a raw nerve of his own. A hint of despair comes through. He ventilates frustration at the ease with which so much arduous labor can be quickly undone. He adds the caveat:

> Because the church is so frail and tender, and so easily overthrown, one must be on constant guard against these fanatics. For when they have heard two sermons or have read a couple of pages in the Sacred Scriptures, they suddenly make themselves masters of all pupils and teachers, contrary to the authority of all men. . . . In fact, even many who think that they understand the doctrine of faith and have been tested by temptation are led astray by them.[6]

What Paul experienced in the first century and Luther in the sixteenth, we are experiencing in our time: a quick and facile departure from the purity of the gospel.

In his article J. I. Packer asks this question: "May ECT *realistically* claim, as in effect it does, that its evangelical and Catholic drafters agree on the gospel of salvation? Yes and no."[7]

Packer asserts that the answer is no with respect to the "small print." He argues that the Tridentine assertion of merit cannot be harmonized with the Reformation assertion of imputed righteousness. The answer is yes in the following respect:

> But if you mean, does ECT's insistence that the Christ of Scripture, creeds, and confessions is faith's proper focus, and that "Christian witness is of necessity aimed at conversion," not only as an initial step but as a personal life-process, and that this constitutes a sufficient account of the gospel of salvation for shared evangelistic ministry, then surely yes. What brings salvation, after all, is not any theory about faith in Christ, justification, and the church, but faith itself in Christ himself. Here also ECT, fairly read, seems to me to pass muster, though the historic disagreements at theory level urgently now need review.[8]

I have read few statements that beg the question more than this one. The first question it begs is this: Which creeds and confessions present Christ and his work as the proper focus of faith? Is Packer thinking of Reformed confessions like the Westminster Confession, the Belgic Confession, and the Heidelberg Catechism? Or does he include in these creeds and confessions the canons and decrees of the Council of Trent, which present a view of Christ's work that is dramatically opposed to the Reformed confessions? Does Trent's view of conversion provide a "sufficient account of the gospel of salvation for shared evangelistic ministry"?

Packer argues that it is faith itself in Christ himself that brings salvation, not any theory about faith in Christ, justification, or the church. This is a red herring. What Reformed person ever asserted that justification is by faith in the doctrine of justification by faith alone? Who has maintained that doctrinal theory ever saved anyone? The sole point of *sola fide,* which Rome categorically rejects, is that we are saved by faith in Jesus Christ alone. The issue is not, Does Christ save or does doctrine save? The issue is, What is the gospel that must be the basis of any shared mission of faith?

All agree that there are saved Christians in the Roman Catholic Church, believers who cling to the biblical Christ, believe the biblical gospel, and trust solely in Christ for their salvation. They are *sola fideists* who believe the gospel in spite of their institution's repudiation of it. And there are multitudes of unsaved people in evangelical churches (including members) who do not believe the gospel that is confessed and preached in these churches.

Packer speaks of faith itself in Christ himself. Still absent is the word *alone*. Can a person be saved if he has faith in Christ and in his own works and merit? Even if we answered yes to this, we are still faced with a deeper question: Can we declare a unity of faith and mission with an institution that anathematizes *sola fide*? We can say yes only if *sola fide* is not essential to the gospel but is merely fine print. If *sola fide* is essential to the gospel, however, then we must answer with a resounding no.

At one point Packer says almost in passing that the Evangelical and Roman Catholic views are "hardly harmonizable" but that the document is good as far as it goes. This comment deeply puzzles me. To say that two views are hardly harmonizable is not the same thing as to say that they are "barely" harmonizable. If two views are different at certain points, they can still be compatible, if only "barely." But if two views are "hardly harmonizable," that normally means they are actually incompatible, and indeed radically incompatible. If Packer considers the two views incompatible, why does he think that the document is good as far as it goes and that it "passes muster"? Only he can answer that.

The One Gospel

With one part of Packer's statement I strongly agree: ". . . the historic disagreements at theory level urgently now need review." Surely the historic disagreements are in need of review—urgent need. The wide acceptance of ECT in the evangelical world fuels that urgency. The salutary benefit of ECT and the resulting controversy is that it has brought the issue of justification back to center stage. The controversy will force everyone, as controversies tend to do, to examine closely the issues involved. It cannot hurt us to focus afresh on the question, What is the gospel?

Paul helps us do this in Galatians 1:7: "Which is not another gospel: only there are some that trouble you, and *would pervert the gospel of Christ*" (ASV, italics mine).

Though Paul earlier spoke of another gospel, here he explains that in reality there is no other gospel. There is only one gospel. Luther sees Paul's reference to "another gospel" as an example of irony. Referring to Satan's ploy of appearing as an angel of light (*sub specie boni*), Luther notes that heretics do not usually call themselves heretics. The heretic passes off his teaching as biblical wherever possible. Luther says: "He peddles his deadly poison as the doctrine of grace, the Word of God, and the Gospel of Christ."[9]

Paul speaks of those who "trouble" the Galatians and "pervert" the gospel. In what sense were the false teachers troubling the Galatians? Ridderbos observes: "To *trouble* means, in this connection, to bring about spiritual schism and an obscuration of the insight of faith."[10]

Luther interprets it in this manner: "He calls them troublers of the churches and of consciences, who do nothing but seduce and deceive an endless number of consciences and cause horrible damage and trouble in the churches. . . . There is always such controversy and condemnation going on in the church, especially when the doctrine of the Gospel is prospering. . . ."[11]

Luther's concern is not unlike Paul's. It is a concern for the flock, the people of God. Luther adds: "Meanwhile the poor common people are confused. They waver back and forth, wondering and doubting which side to take or whom it is safe to follow."[12]

The problems faced by the troubled ones in Galatia were compounded by the false teachers' competence and giftedness. The false teachers did not appear as sheep in wolves' clothing. It was the reverse. Again Luther remarks: "For if the false apostles had not possessed outstanding gifts, great authority, and the appearance of holiness; and if they had not claimed to be the ministers of Christ, pupils of the apostles, and sincere preachers of the Gospel, they could not so easily have undermined the authority of Paul and made an impression on the Galatians."[13]

Paul uses strong words in denouncing the false teachers, charging them with perverting the gospel. The word *pervert* here carries the idea of "destroying," for a perverted gospel destroys the true gospel. Calvin notes:

> He charges them with the second crime of doing an injury to Christ by wanting to destroy His Gospel. And this is a very dreadful crime; for destruction is worse than corruption. And with good reason does he accuse them. When the glory of justifying man is transferred to another and a snare is set for consciences, the Saviour no longer stands firm and the teaching of the Gospel is ruined. For we must always take care of the main articles of the Gospel. He who attacks them is a destroyer of the Gospel.[14]

In Galatians 1:8 Paul's polemic reaches a crescendo. To emphasize the gravity of the issue, the apostle offers a hypothetical scenario: "But though we, or an angel from heaven, should preach unto you any gospel other than that which we preached unto you, let him be anathema" (ASV).

We regard as unthinkable the hypothesis of Paul preaching another gospel, because we believe Paul wrote under the inspiration of the Holy Spirit and was an agent of divine revelation. In church history we see dramatic shifts in theologians' teaching, so we distinguish between "early" Augustine and "later" Augustine (à la his *Retractiones*) and between early Berkouwer and later Berkouwer. We do this to accommodate changes in their thinking.

But Paul said that if by some means he should ever alter the gospel he had already preached, God should curse him.

Then Paul mentions the hypothetical case of another gospel being proclaimed by an angel from heaven. Paul knew full well that the only angel who would pervert the gospel would come from hell, not heaven. Paul may be indulging in hyperbole, but his point is clear. *If anyone. . . .* That is the point. No one, not even an angel, is to be tolerated if he preaches "another" gospel. Status, credentials, authority, prior credibility: they all mean nothing if one is preaching a different gospel. Calvin observes: "And thus when he pronounces a judgment of anathema on angels if they should teach anything else, though he argues from an impossibility, it is not superfluous. For this exaggeration helped to increase the authority of Paul's preaching. He saw that he and his teaching were attacked by the use of famous names. He replies that not even angels have the weight to overwhelm it. This is no insult to the angels."[15]

The harshest point made by Paul is the penalty he calls for on those who preach a different gospel. It is not mere rebuke, censure, or admonition. It is anathema or curse. Nor is this penalty left solely to God; it is also to be expressed by the church. It is even stronger than excommunication. Luther says: "Here Paul is breathing fire.... This is a passionate zeal, that he has the courage to curse so boldly not only himself and his brethren but even an angel from heaven. The Greek word *anathema* ... means something cursed, execrable, contemptible, something that has no relation, participation, or communication with God."[16]

In case this pronouncement of the curse is not enough, Paul moves on to repeat himself, a Hebrew literary device to communicate strong emphasis: "As we have said before, so say I now again, If any man preacheth unto you any gospel other than that which you [have] received, let him be anathema" (1:9 ASV).

This repetition is almost verbatim. One small change, however, requires comment. In verse 8 Paul utters the anathema on himself and on angels. In verse 9 he makes it universal, applying the anathema to anyone who preaches another gospel.

The Question of Motivation

Paul then turns his attention to the question of his own motives in the controversy: "For am I now seeking the favor of men, or of God? Or am I striving to please men? If I were still pleasing men, I should not be a servant of Christ" (1:10 ASV).

The apostle who penned these words is the same person who was willing to be all things to all men and who was determined, as much as humanly possible, to live at peace with all. But Paul found it impossible to be at peace with those who pervert the gospel. In this controversy over the nature of the gospel and of justification, Paul was unwilling to be a man-pleaser. He had no time for the politics of compromise when it came to the gospel.

He found himself in a situation where he could not faithfully serve Christ and please men.

Luther remarks: "I declare that they do not become righteous by works or by circumcision but solely by grace and by faith in Christ. Because this is what I preach, I earn the bitter hatred of men. . . . Whoever tries to please God will have men as his bitter enemies."[17]

Calvin adds: "When there reigns in our hearts such ambition that we want to frame our speech so as to please men, we cannot teach sincerely. . . . Whereas those who want true doctrine to give place to their own purposes are on no account to be gratified."[18]

Any minister who has ever refused to compromise the gospel at any point has felt the rage and invective of his opponents *and* his friends. This was true of Paul, Luther, Calvin, Edwards, and every other servant of Christ who has remained faithful to Christ and his gospel. They have been called bigoted, obstreperous, divisive, intolerant, and a host of other insulting things. Their character and reputations have been viciously attacked. But they have followed their Savior in being willing to lose their reputations, indeed to have no reputation, if loyalty to God demanded it.

To be sure there resides in all of us a tendency toward obstinancy and a resistance to being proven wrong. Such an uncompromising spirit is of the flesh and is no virtue. To remain obstinate and unyielding in error is a sin. To be uncompromising with the truth of the gospel is a virtue and is demanded of all who would be servants of Christ.

Paul is uncompromising in his teaching of the gospel, not because it is his gospel or his doctrine or his opinion. He refuses to compromise because the gospel for which he contends is the gospel of Christ. It is not merely a gospel *about* Christ, it is the gospel *from* Christ: "For I make known to you, brethren, as touching the gospel which was preached by me, that it is not after man. For neither did I receive it from man, nor was I taught it, but it came to me through revelation of Jesus Christ" (1:11–12 ASV).

The current collapse of Evangelicalism could be a good thing if historic evangelical theology were a distortion of the gospel of Christ. If historic Evangelicalism did hold the true gospel, then its current weakening is a major calamity for the church. In *Chris-*

tianity Today J. I. Packer spoke of the fear that was motivating opponents of ECT: ". . . I ought to have anticipated that some Protestants would say bleak, skewed, fearful, and fear-driven things about this document—for instance, that it betrays the Reformation. . . ."[19]

Packer graciously declined to name names. I don't know how many people said that ECT "betrayed the Reformation." I said in print that it "trivialized the Reformation." I also said elsewhere that it betrayed the Reformation, as I believe it did.

But far more important is the question of betraying the gospel. It is easy for me to fall into the trap of idealizing the Reformation. I do believe that the heart of the Reformation was the recovery and heroic defense of the gospel of *sola fide*. My loyalty to the Reformers, however, cannot justify my opposition to ECT if it is correct in affirming a unified faith. No church tradition can bind the conscience. But the Word of God must bind the conscience and take precedence over any and all other loyalties.

Surely this was a major concern to Paul. The Judaizer heresy of his day so threatened the unity of Christ's body that it necessitated a confrontation between Paul and Peter himself. Who had higher credentials than Peter? Yet the Apostle Peter was in danger of compromising the gospel. In Galatians 2 Paul provides the following account:

> But when Cephas came to Antioch, I resisted him to the face, because he stood condemned. For before that certain came from James, he ate with the Gentiles; but when they came, he drew back and separated himself, fearing them that were of the circumcision. And the rest of the Jews dissembled likewise with him; insomuch that even Barnabas was carried away with their dissimulation. But when I saw that they walked not uprightly according to the truth of the gospel, I said unto Cephas before them all, If thou, being a Jew, livest as do the Gentiles, and not as do the Jews, how compellest thou the Gentiles to live as do the Jews? (Gal. 2:11–14 ASV)

This incident that so threatened apostolic unity concerned the gospel in its pure expression. Paul gives the motive and rationale for confronting Peter:

> We being Jews by nature, and not sinners of the Gentiles, yet knowing that a man is not justified by the works of the law but through faith in Jesus Christ, even we believed on Christ Jesus, that we might be justified by faith in Christ, and not by the works of the law: because by the works of the law shall no flesh be justified. (Gal. 2:15–16 ASV)

Paul rebuked Peter publicly because his offense had been a public one. As we learn from the rest of Scripture, Peter accepted the correction and humbly, obediently returned to a lifelong defense of the gospel. Calvin argued that had Paul remained silent on this matter, his whole teaching would have fallen: "This was no human business matter but involved the purity of the Gospel, which was in danger of being contaminated by Jewish leaven."[20]

Calvin noted Roman Catholic attempts to see this dispute as one about mere ceremonies:

> For they see no absurdity in maintaining that no man is justified by the works of the law and yet also that we are accounted righteous in the sight of God by the merits of works. In short, they hold that this does not refer to moral works. But the context shows clearly that the moral law is also comprehended in these words, for almost everything that Paul adds relates to the moral rather than the ceremonial law. Then again, he continually contrasts the righteousness of the law to the free acceptance with which God is pleased to favour us.[21]

Calvin's concluding summary of this section of Galatians may serve also as a concluding summary for this book: "Let it therefore remain settled that this proposition is exclusive, that we are justified in no other way than by faith, or, which comes to the same thing, that we are justified by faith alone."[22]

Sola gratia
Sola fide
Soli Deo gloria

Notes

Foreword

1. Quoted in *Berean Call* (September 1994).

2. For instance, in *Christian Spirituality: Five Views of Sanctification*, Russell Spittler (of Fuller Theological Seminary), Lawrence Wood (Asbury Theological Seminary), and Glenn Hinson (Southern Baptist Seminary) all represent positions concerning justification and sanctification that are more in line with medieval Roman Catholicism than with Reformation Christianity. Reflecting the Pelagian tendencies within Pentecostalism, Spittler says that Luther's teaching concerning justification "looks wrong to me." "I hope it's true!" writes Spittler. "I simply fear it's not" (p. 43). Only Sinclair Ferguson (Westminster Theological Seminary) and Gerhard Forde (Luther-Northwestern Theological Seminary) take the traditional evangelical position. Donald L. Alexander, ed., *Christian Spirituality: Five Views of Sanctification* (Downers Grove, Ill.: InterVarsity, 1988).

Chapter 1, Light in the Darkness

1. Harold Lindsell, *The Battle for the Bible* (Grand Rapids: Zondervan, 1976).

2. For a more complete survey of this debate, see R. Alan Day, *Lordship: What Does It Mean?* (Nashville: Broadman, 1993); Kenneth L. Gentry Jr., *Lord of the Saved: Getting to the Heart of the Lordship Debate* (Phillipsburg, N.J.: P & R, 1992); Zane C. Hodges, *Absolutely Free! A Biblical Reply to Lordship Salvation* (Grand Rapids, Mich.: Zondervan, 1989); and John F. MacArthur Jr., *Faith Works* (Dallas: Word, 1993).

3. *Evangelicals and Catholics Together: The Christian Mission in the Third Millennium*, released March 29, 1994. Available from BASIC Truth Ministries, P.O. Box 504M, Bay Shore, NY 11706. Also printed in *First Things* (May 1994): 15–22.

4. Ibid., p. 1.

5. Ibid.

6. Ibid., p. 2.

7. Ibid., p. 5.

8. Henricus Denzinger, ed., *Enchiridion symbolorum: Definitionum et declarationum de rebus fidei et morum*, 32d ed. (Barcelona: Herder, 1963), p. 577.

Chapter 2, Evangelicals and Catholics: Together or in Dialogue?

1. *Evangelicals and Catholics Together: The Christian Mission in the Third Millennium*, p. 5.

2. Ibid., p. 10.

3. Ibid.

4. Ibid., p. 8.

5. Ibid., p. 9.

6. *Resolutions for Roman Catholic and Evangelical Dialogue* is available from Christians United for Reformation, 2568 E. Riles Circle, Anaheim, CA 92806. Also printed in *Modern Reformation* (July 1994): 28–29.

7. *Evangelicals and Catholics Together*, pp. 11–12.

8. *Resolutions for Roman Catholic and Evangelical Dialogue*, p. 1. Italics mine.

9. Ibid., p. 2.

Chapter 3, Watershed at Worms

1. Henricus Denzinger, ed., *Enchiridion symbolorum: Definitionum et declarationum de rebus fidei et morum* (Barcelona: Herder, 1964), pp. 357–58.

2. Clyde L. Manschreck, ed., *A History of Christianity: Readings in the History of the Church*, vol. 2, *The Church from the Reformation to the Present* (Grand Rapids, Mich.: Baker, 1981), p. 29.

3. Harold J. Grimm, *The Reformation Era: 1500–1650* (New York: Macmillan, 1954), p. 137.

4. Gordon Rupp, *Luther's Progress to the Diet of Worms* (New York: Harper and Row, 1964), p. 95.

5. Ibid., p. 94.

6. Ibid., p. 95. The first letter quoted was dated April 7, 1521; the second, April 14, 1521.

7. Manschreck, ed., *A History of Christianity*, 2:29.

8. Heiko A. Oberman, *Luther: Man between God and the Devil*, trans. Eileen Walliser-Schwarzbart (New Haven: Yale University, 1989), p. 38.

9. Ibid.

10. Rupp, *Luther's Progress*, p. 96.

11. Manschreck, ed., *A History of Christianity*, 2:52–53.

12. Ibid., 2:29–30.

13. Ibid., 2:31.

14. Ibid.

15. Rupp, *Luther's Progress*, p. 98.

16. Manschreck, ed., *A History of Christianity*, 2:32.

17. Ibid.

18. Roland H. Bainton, *Here I Stand: A Life of Martin Luther* (New York: New American Library, 1955), p. 64.

19. Ibid., p. 15.

20. Rupp, *Luther's Progress*, p. 23.

21. Manschreck, ed., *A History of Christianity*, 2:4.

22. Bainton, *Here I Stand*, pp. 49–50.

23. Rupp, *Luther's Progress*, p. 51.

24. Grimm, *The Reformation Era*, p. 107.

25. Rupp, *Luther's Progress*, p. 51.

26. Manschreck, ed., *A History of Christianity*, 2:5.

27. Oberman, *Luther*, p. 188.

28. Grimm, *The Reformation Era*, p. 109.

29. Manschreck, ed., *A History of Christianity*, 2:15.

30. Oberman, *Luther*, pp. 190–91.

31. Ibid., p. 191.

32. Manschreck, ed., *A History of Christianity*, 2:19.

33. Oberman, *Luther*, p. 196.

34. Rupp, *Luther's Progress*, p. 69.

Chapter 4, Justification and Faith

1. Martin Luther, *What Luther Says: An Anthology*, ed. Ewald M. Plass, 3 vols. (St. Louis: Concordia, 1959), 2:704 n.5.

2. Ibid., 2:703.

3. Ibid.

4. John Calvin, *Institutes of the Christian Religion*, 2 vols., trans. Henry Beveridge (1845; reprint, Grand Rapids, Mich.: Eerdmans, 1964), 2:37 (3.11.1).

5. J. I. Packer, "Introductory Essay," in James Buchanan, *The Doctrine of Justification: An Outline of Its History in the Church and of Its Exposition from Scripture* (London: Banner of Truth, 1961), p. vii.

6. Ibid., pp. viii, ix.

7. Ayn Rand, *Atlas Shrugged* (New York: Random, 1957).

8. Luther, *What Luther Says*, 2:710–11.

9. Ibid., 1: 465.

10. Herman Witsius, *Sacred Dissertations on What Is Commonly Called the Apostles' Creed*, trans. Donald Fraser, 2 vols. (1823; reprint, Phillipsburg, N.J.: P & R, 1993), 1:42–43.

11. Francis Turretin, *Institutes of Elenctic Theology*, vol. 2, *Eleventh through Seventeenth Topics*, trans. George Musgrave Giger, ed. James T. Dennison Jr. (Phillipsburg, N.J.: P & R, 1994), p. 561.

12. Luther, *What Luther Says*, 1:474.

13. Ibid., 1:487.

14. Ibid., 1:487–88.

15. Jonathan Edwards, *Freedom of the Will* (1754; reprint, New Haven: Yale University, 1957).

16. Turretin, *Institutes of Elenctic Theology*, 2:562.

17. Ibid.

18. Witsius, *Sacred Dissertations*, 1:48.

19. Turretin, *Institutes of Elenctic Theology*, 2:562.

20. Witsius, *Sacred Dissertations*, 1:49.

21. Turretin, *Institutes of Elenctic Theology*, 2:563.

22. Witsius, *Sacred Dissertations*, 1:51.

23. Turretin, *Institutes of Elenctic Theology*, 2:563.

24. Witsius, *Sacred Dissertations*, 1:57.

25. Ibid.

Chapter 5, Imputed Righteousness: The Evangelical Doctrine

1. *Canons and Decrees of the Council of Trent: Original Text with English Translation*, trans. H. J. Schroeder (London: Herder, 1941), p. 33.

2. Alister E. McGrath, *Iustitia Dei: A History of the Christian Doctrine of Justification*, 2 vols. (Cambridge: Cambridge University, 1986), 1:9.

3. Ibid., 1:2.

4. Ibid., 1:30–31.

5. Ibid., 1:31.

6. James Buchanan, *The Doctrine of Justification: An Outline of Its History in the Church and of Its Exposition from Scripture* (1867; reprint, London: Banner of Truth, 1961), p. 226.

7. Ibid., pp. 226–27.

8. Francis Turretin, *Institutes of Elenctic Theology*, vol. 2, *Eleventh through Seventeenth Topics*, trans. George Musgrave Giger, ed. James T. Dennison Jr. (Phillipsburg, N.J.: P & R, 1994), p. 634.

9. John Calvin, *Institutes of the Christian Religion*, 2 vols., trans. Henry Beveridge (1845; reprint, Grand Rapids, Mich.: Eerdmans, 1964), 2:37 (3.11.1).

10. Ibid., 2:37–38 (3.11.2).

11. Ibid., 2:38 (3.11.2).

12. Ibid.

13. Ibid., 2:39 (3.11.3).

14. Ibid.

15. Turretin, *Institutes of Elenctic Theology*, 2:647.

16. Ibid., 2:651.

17. Calvin, *Institutes of the Christian Religion*, 2:58 (3.11.23).

18. G. C. Berkouwer, *Geloof en Rechtvaardiging*, Dogmatische Studiën (Kampen: Kok, 1949), pp. 87–88. Translation mine. See also *Faith and Justification*, trans. Lewis B. Smedes, Studies in Dogmatics (Grand Rapids, Mich.: Eerdmans, 1954), pp. 87–88.

19. Buchanan, *The Doctrine of Justification*, pp. 334–35.

20. Ibid., p. 318.

21. Ibid., p. 326.

22. Berkouwer, *Geloof en Rechtvaardiging*, p. 92. Translation mine. See also *Faith and Justification*, p. 91.

23. Alister E. McGrath, *Justification by Faith: What It Means for Us Today* (London: Marshall Pickering / Grand Rapids, Mich.: Zondervan, 1988), p. 61.

24. John H. Gerstner, "Aquinas Was a Protestant," *Tabletalk* 18 (May 1994): 52. Michael Root, "Alister McGrath on Cross and Justification," *The Thomist* 54 (October 1990): 710.

25. Gerstner, "Aquinas Was a Protestant," pp. 14–15. Kenneth J. Foreman, "Soteriology," in Lefferts A. Loetscher, ed., *Twentieth Century Encyclopedia of Religious Knowledge*, 2 vols. (Grand Rapids, Mich.: Baker, 1955), 2:1050.

26. McGrath, *Justification by Faith*, p. 71.

Chapter 6, Infused Righteousness: The Catholic Doctrine

1. Hans Küng, *Rechtfertigung: Die Lehre Karl Barths und eine katholische Besinnung* (Einsiedeln: Johannes, 1957), p. 109. Translation mine. ("*Die allermeisten dogmatischen Definitionen sind* polemische Formeln, *ausgesprochen gegen Häresien, Verteidigungsdämme gegen den Irrtum. . . .*")

2. G. C. Berkouwer, *Vatikaans Concilie en Nieuwe Theologie* (Kampen: Kok, 1964), p. 231. Cf. *The Second Vatican Council and the New Catholicism*, trans. Lewis B. Smedes (Grand Rapids, MIch.: Eerdmans, 1965), p. 188.

3. Berkouwer, *Vatikaans Concilie*, p. 235. Cf. *The Second Vatican Council*, p. 191.

4. *Canons and Decrees of the Council of Trent: Original Text with English Translation,* trans. H. J. Schroeder (London: Herder, 1941), p. 31. Italics mine.

5. Berkouwer, *Vatikaans Concilie*, p. 239; *The Second Vatican Council*, p. 194.

6. *Canons and Decrees of the Council of Trent*, pp. 21ff.

7. Ibid., pp. 34–35.

8. Ibid., p. 313.

9. Ibid., p. 39.

10. *Catechism of the Catholic Church* (Liguori, Mo.: Liguori, 1994), p. 482, par. 1992.

11. *Canons and Decrees of the Council of Trent*, p. 40.

12. John Calvin, *Acts of the Council of Trent: With the Antidote*, ed. and trans. Henry Beveridge (1851), in *Selected Works of John Calvin: Tracts and Letters*, ed. Henry Beveridge and Jules Bonnet, 7 vols. (Grand Rapids, Mich.: Baker, 1983), 3:121–22. Italics mine.

13. Ibid., 3:122.

14. *Canons and Decrees of the Council of Trent*, p. 41.

15. *Evangelicals and Catholics Together: The Christian Mission in the Third Millennium* (1994), p. 5.

16. *Canons and Decrees of the Council of Trent*, p. 41.

17. Ibid., p. 42.

18. Ibid., p. 43.

19. Calvin, *Acts of the Council of Trent*, 3:152.

20. *Canons and Decrees of the Council of Trent*, p. 43.

21. Calvin, *Acts of the Council of Trent*, 3:151.

22. *Canons and Decrees of the Council of Trent*, p. 43.

23. Calvin, *Acts of the Council of Trent*, 3:151–52.

24. *Canons and Decrees of the Council of Trent*, p. 270.

Chapter 7, Merit and Grace

1. Adolph Harnack, *History of Dogma*, 7 vols., trans. James Millar (New York: Dover, 1961), 5:173.

2. Ibid., 5:175.

3. Ibid., 5:204–5.

4. Thomas Aquinas, *Nature and Grace: Selections from the "Summa theologica" of Thomas Aquinas*, ed. and trans. A. M. Fairweather, Library of Christian Classics, vol. 11 (London: SCM / Philadelphia: Westminster, 1954), pp. 137–56. *Summa theologica*, 12ae, Q. 109, Art. 1–10.

5. Thomas Aquinas, *Nature and Grace*, p. 157. *Summa theologica*, 12ae, Q. 110, Art. 1.

6. Thomas Aquinas, *Nature and Grace*, p. 167. *Summa theologica*, 12ae, Q. 111, Art. 2.

7. Thomas Aquinas, *Nature and Grace*, p. 169. *Summa theologica*, 12ae, Q. 111, Art. 3.

8. *Canons and Decrees of the Council of Trent: Original Text with English Translation,* trans. H. J. Schroeder (London: Herder, 1941), pp. 31–32.

9. G. C. Berkouwer, *The Conflict with Rome,* trans. David H. Freeman (Philadelphia: Presbyterian and Reformed, 1958), p. 77. Cf. Herman Bavinck, *Gereformeerde Dogmatiek*, 2d ed., 4 vols. (1911), 3:509.

10. Berkouwer, *The Conflict with Rome*, p. 80.

11. Ibid., p. 82.

12. Ibid., p. 84. Cf. John Calvin, *Institutes of the Christian Religion*, 2.2.7.

13. *Catechism of the Catholic Church* (Liguori, Mo.: Liguori, 1994), p. 485, par. 2003.

14. See G. C. Berkouwer, *Verdienste of Genade? Rede ter Gelegenheid van de Achten-zeventigste Herdenking van de Stichting der Vrije Universiteit op Maandag 20 Oktober 1958 Uitgesproken door de Rector Magnificus* (Kampen: Kok, 1958), pp. 22–24.

15. John Calvin, *Acts of the Council of Trent: With the Antidote,* ed. and trans. Henry Beveridge (1851), in *Selected Works of John Calvin: Tracts and Letters,* ed. Henry Beveridge and Jules Bonnet, 7 vols. (Grand Rapids, Mich.: Baker, 1983), 3:111. Augustine, *On the Merits and Forgiveness of Sins* and *On Rebuke and Grace.*

16. Calvin, *Acts of the Council of Trent,* 3:113.

17. Berkouwer, *Verdienste of Genade?* p. 38.

18. *Catechism of the Catholic Church,* p. 370, par. 1471.

19. Ibid. First paragraph quoted from Paul VI, apostolic constitution, *Indulgentiarum doctrina,* Norm 1; second paragraph (first sentence) quoted from ibid., Norm 2.

20. *Catechism of the Catholic Church,* p. 370, par. 1472.

21. Ibid., p. 371, pars. 1475–76.

22. Ibid., p. 371, par. 1477. Quoted from Paul VI, apostolic constitution, *Indulgentiarum doctrina,* 5.

23. *Canons and Decrees of the Council of Trent,* pp. 90–91.

24. Ibid., p. 97.

25. Ibid.

26. Ibid., p. 98.

27. Ibid.

28. Ibid.

29. Calvin, *Acts of the Council of Trent,* 3:140–41.

30. Donald Bloesch, "Is Spirituality Enough? Differing Models for Living," in John Armstrong, ed., *Roman Catholicism: Evangelical Protestants Analyze What Divides and Unites Us* (Chicago: Moody, 1994), p. 151.

31. John Calvin, *The Epistles of Paul the Apostle to the Galatians, Ephesians, Philippians and Colossians,* ed. David W. Torrance and Thomas F. Torrance, trans. T. H. L. Parker (Edinburgh: Oliver and Boyd / Grand Rapids, Mich.: Eerdmans, 1965), p. 125. A comment on Eph. 1:4.

32. James Buchanan, *The Doctrine of Justification: An Outline of Its History in the Church and of Its Exposition from Scripture* (1867; reprint, London: Banner of Truth, 1961), p. 90.

33. *Catechism of the Catholic Church,* p. 486, pars. 2007–8.

34. Ibid., p. 487, par. 2009. Quotation from Augustine, *Sermons* 298.4–5.

35. Thomas Aquinas, *Nature and Grace,* p. 207. *Summa theologica,* 12ae, Q. 114, Art. 3.

36. Hans Küng, *Rechtfertigung: Die Lehre Karl Barths und eine katholische Besinnung* (Einsiedeln: Johannes, 1957), p. 263.

37. Martin Luther, *What Luther Says: An Anthology,* ed. Ewald M. Plass, 3 vols. (St. Louis: Concordia, 1959), 2:921.

38. Ibid., 2:922.

39. John Calvin, *Institutes of the Christian Religion,* 2 vols., trans. Henry Beveridge (1845; reprint, Grand Rapids, Mich.: Eerdmans, 1964), 2:91 (3.15.2).

Chapter 8, Faith and Works

1. *Canons and Decrees of the Council of Trent: Original Text with English Translation,* trans. H. J. Schroeder (London: Herder, 1941), p. 45.

2. John Calvin, *Acts of the Council of Trent: With the Antidote*, ed. and trans. Henry Beveridge (1851), in *Selected Works of John Calvin: Tracts and Letters*, ed. Henry Beveridge and Jules Bonnet, 7 vols. (Grand Rapids, Mich.: Baker, 1983), 3:158.

3. *Canons and Decrees of the Council of Trent*, p. 46.

4. Calvin, *Acts of the Council of Trent*, 3:162.

5. Martin Luther, *What Luther Says: An Anthology*, ed. Ewald M. Plass, 3 vols. (St. Louis: Concordia, 1959), 3:1507.

6. *Canons and Decrees of the Council of Trent*, p. 45.

7. Calvin, *Acts of the Council of Trent*, 3:158.

8. John Calvin, *Institutes of the Christian Religion*, 2 vols., trans. Henry Beveridge (1845; reprint, Grand Rapids, Mich.: Eerdmans, 1964), 2:98–99 (3.16.1).

9. Ibid., 2:99 (3.16.1).

10. *Canons and Decrees of the Council of Trent*, p. 36.

11. Calvin, *Institutes of the Christian Religion*, 2:55 (3.11.19).

12. Ibid.

13. Luther, *What Luther Says*, 2:707–8.

14. G. C. Berkouwer, *Geloof en Rechtvaardiging*, Dogmatische Studiën (Kampen: Kok, 1949), p. 131. Translation mine. See also *Faith and Justification*, trans. Lewis B. Smedes, Studies in Dogmatics (Grand Rapids, Mich.: Eerdmans, 1954), p. 131.

15. Calvin, *Institutes of the Christian Religion*, 2:114 (3.17.11).

16. Ibid., 2:115 (3.17.12).

17. Gottlob Schrenk, "*Dikaiosynē*," *Theological Dictionary of the New Testament*, ed. Gerhard Kittel, trans. and ed. Geoffrey W. Bromiley, vol. 2 (Grand Rapids, Mich.: Eerdmans, 1964), p. 201.

18. Zane C. Hodges, *Absolutely Free! A Biblical Reply to Lordship Salvation* (Grand Rapids, Mich.: Zondervan, 1989), p. 125.

19. Zane C. Hodges, *Dead Faith: What Is It?* (Dallas: Redención Viva, 1987), p. 7. Quoted in John F. MacArthur Jr., *Faith Works: The Gospel According to the Apostles* (Dallas: Word, 1993), p. 155, n. 25.

20. D. A. Carson, *Exegetical Fallacies* (Grand Rapids, Mich.: Baker, 1984), p. 137. Quoted in MacArthur, *Faith Works*, p. 155 n. 25.

21. Alexander Ross, *The Epistles of James and John*, New International Commentary on the New Testament (Grand Rapids, Mich.: Eerdmans, 1954), p. 53 n. 12. A comment on James 2:20.

22. Calvin, *Institutes of the Christian Religion*, 2:115 (3.17.12).

23. Charles Hodge, *A Commentary on Romans*, rev. ed. (1909; reprint, London: Banner of Truth, 1972), p. 100. A comment on Romans 3:28.

24. Ibid.

25. Charles C. Ryrie, *So Great Salvation: What It Means to Believe in Jesus Christ* (Wheaton, Ill.: Victor, 1989), p. 45.

26. Hodges, *Absolutely Free!* p. 160.

27. Ibid., p. 145. Calvin, *Institutes of the Christian Religion*, 3.3.5.

28. Calvin, *Institutes of the Christian Religion*, 1:509–10 (3.3.1).

29. Ibid., 1:509 (3.3.1).

30. Ibid., 1:512 (3.3.5).

31. Hodges, *Absolutely Free!* pp. 145–46.

Chapter 9, No Other Gospel

1. Herman N. Ridderbos, *The Epistle of Paul to the Churches of Galatia*, trans. Henry Zylstra, New International Commentary on the New Testament (Grand Rapids, Mich.: Eerdmans, 1953), p. 46. A comment on Gal. 1:6–9.

2. Martin Luther, *Lectures on Galatians (1535)*, ed. and trans. Jaroslav Pelikan, 2 vols., *Luther's Works*, vols. 26–27 (St. Louis: Concordia: 1963–64), 26:44. A comment on Gal. 1:6.

3. John Calvin, *The Epistles of Paul the Apostle to the Galatians, Ephesians, Philippians, and Colossians*, ed. David W. Torrance and Thomas F. Torrance, trans. T. H. L. Parker (Edinburgh: Oliver and Boyd / Grand Rapids, Mich.: Eerdmans, 1965), p. 13. A comment on Gal. 1:6.

4. Ridderbos, *The Epistle of Paul to the Churches of Galatia*, p. 47. A comment on Gal. 1:6.

5. Luther, *Lectures on Galatians*, LW 26:45. A comment on Gal. 1:6.

6. Ibid., 26:45–46. A comment on Gal. 1:6.

7. J. I. Packer, "Why I Signed It," *Christianity Today*, 12 December 1994, pp. 36–37. Italics mine.

8. Ibid., p. 37.

9. Luther, *Lectures on Galatians*, LW 26:49. A comment on Gal. 1:6.

10. Ridderbos, *The Epistle of Paul to the Churches of Galatia*, p. 49. A comment on Gal. 1:7.

11. Luther, *Lectures on Galatians*, LW 26:51. A comment on Gal. 1:7.

12. Ibid.

13. Ibid., 26:52. A comment on Gal. 1:7.

14. Calvin, *The Epistles of Paul the Apostle*, p. 14. A comment on Gal. 1:7.

15. Ibid., p. 15. A comment on Gal. 1:8.

16. Luther, *Lectures on Galatians*, LW 26:55. A comment on Gal. 1:8.

17. Ibid., 26:59–60. A comment on Gal. 1:10.

18. Calvin, *The Epistles of Paul the Apostle*, p. 17. A comment on Gal. 1:10.

19. Packer, "Why I Signed It," p. 34.

20. Calvin, *The Epistles of Paul the Apostle*, p. 36. A comment on Gal. 2:14.

21. Ibid., p. 38. A comment on Gal. 2:15.

22. Ibid., p. 39. A comment on Gal. 2:16.

Bibliography

Armstrong, John, ed. *Roman Catholicism: Evangelical Protestants Analyze What Divides and Unites Us.* Chicago: Moody, 1994.

Barrett, C. K. *A Commentary on the Epistle to the Romans.* Black's New Testament Commentaries. London: Black, 1957. Harper's New Testament Commentaries. New York: Harper, 1957.

Berkouwer, G. C. *The Conflict with Rome.* Translated by David H. Freeman. Philadelphia: Presbyterian and Reformed, 1958.

———. *Geloof en Rechtvaardiging.* Dogmatische Studiën. Kampen: Kok, 1949. English translation: *Faith and Justification.* Translated by Lewis B. Smedes. Studies in Dogmatics. Grand Rapids, Mich.: Eerdmans, 1954.

———. *Nabetrachting op het Concilie.* Kampen: Kok, 1968.

———. *Vatikaans Concilie en Nieuwe Theologie.* Kampen: Kok, 1964. English translation: *The Second Vatican Council and the New Catholicism.* Translated by Lewis B. Smedes. Grand Rapids, Mich.: Eerdmans, 1965.

———. *Verdienste of Genade? Rede ter Gelegenheid van de Achtenzeventigste Herdenking van de Stichting der Vrije Universiteit op Maandag 20 Oktober 1958 Uitgesproken Door de Rector Magnificus.* Kampen: Kok, 1958.

Black, Matthew. *Romans: Based on the Revised Standard Version.* 2d ed. London: Marshall, Morgan, and Scott / Grand Rapids, Mich.: Eerdmans, 1989.

Buchanan, James. *The Doctrine of Justification: An Outline of Its History in the Church and of Its Exposition from Scripture.* 1867. Reprint ed. Grand Rapids, Mich.: Baker, 1955. London: Banner of Truth, 1961.

Calvin, John. *Acts of the Council of Trent: With the Antidote.* Edited and translated by Henry Beveridge. 1851. Reprint ed. *Selected Works of John Calvin: Tracts and Letters.* Edited by Henry Beveridge and Jules Bonnet. 7 vols. Grand Rapids, Mich.: Baker, 1983. 3:17–188.

———. *The Epistles of Paul the Apostle to the Galatians, Ephesians, Philippians and Colossians.* Edited by David W. Torrance and Thomas F. Torrance. Translated by T. H. L. Parker. Edinburgh: Oliver and Boyd / Grand Rapids, Mich.: Eerdmans, 1965.

---. *The Epistles of Paul the Apostle to the Romans and to the Thessalonians.* Edited by David W. Torrance and Thomas F. Torrance. Translated by Ross Mackenzie. Edinburgh: Oliver and Boyd / Grand Rapids, Mich.: Eerdmans, 1961.

---. *Institutes of the Christian Religion.* Translated by Henry Beveridge. 2 vols. 1845. Reprint ed. Grand Rapids, Mich.: Eerdmans, 1964.

Canons and Decrees of the Council of Trent: Original Text with English Translation. Translated by H. J. Schroeder. London: Herder, 1941.

Catechism of the Catholic Church. Liguori, Mo.: Liguori, 1994.

Day, R. Alan. *Lordship: What Does It Mean?* Nashville: Broadman, 1993.

Denzinger, Henricus, ed. *Enchiridion symbolorum: Definitionum et declarationum de rebus fidei et morum.* 32d ed. Barcelona: Herder, 1963.

Dodd, C. H. *The Epistle of Paul to the Romans.* Moffatt New Testament Commentary. London: Hodder and Stoughton, 1932.

Gentry, Kenneth L., Jr. *Lord of the Saved: Getting to the Heart of the Lordship Debate.* Phillipsburg, N.J.: P & R, 1992.

Gerstner, John H. "Aquinas Was a Protestant." *Tabletalk* 18 (May 1994): 12–15, 52.

---. *The Rational Biblical Theology of Jonathan Edwards.* 3 vols. Powhatan, Va.: Berea / Orlando: Ligonier, 1991–92.

Grimm, Harold J. *The Reformation Era: 1500–1650.* New York: Macmillan / London: Collier-Macmillan, 1954.

Harnack, Adolph. *History of Dogma.* 7 vols. Translated by James Millar. New York: Dover, 1961.

Hodge, Charles. *Commentary on the Epistle to the Romans.* Rev. ed. 1909. Reprint ed. London: Banner of Truth, 1972.

Hodges, Zane C. *Absolutely Free! A Biblical Reply to Lordship Salvation.* Grand Rapids, Mich.: Zondervan, 1989.

Kistler, Don, ed. *Justification by Faith Alone: Affirming the Doctrine by which the Church and the Individual Stands or Falls.* Morgan, Pa.: Soli Deo Gloria, 1995.

Küng, Hans. *Infallible? An Inquiry.* Translated by Edward Quinn. Garden City, N.Y.: Doubleday, 1971.

---. *Rechtfertigung: Die Lehre Karl Barths und eine katholische Besinnung.* Einsiedeln: Johannes, 1957.

Luther, Martin. *Lectures on Galatians (1535).* Edited and translated by Jaroslav Pelikan. 2 vols. *Luther's Works,* vols. 26–27. St. Louis: Concordia, 1963–64.

---. *Lectures on Genesis.* Edited by Jaroslav Pelikan. Translated by George V. Schick and Paul D. Pahl. 8 vols. *Luther's Works,* vols. 1-8. St. Louis: Concordia, 1958–70.

---. *What Luther Says: An Anthology.* Edited by Ewald M. Plass. 3 vols. St. Louis: Concordia, 1959.

MacArthur, John F., Jr. *Faith Works: The Gospel According to the Apostles.* Dallas: Word, 1993.

McGrath, Alister E. *Iustitia Dei: A History of the Christian Doctrine of Justification*. 2 vols. Cambridge: Cambridge University, 1986.

————. *Justification by Faith: What It Means for Us Today*. London: Marshall Pickering / Grand Rapids, Mich.: Zondervan, 1988.

Manschreck, Clyde L., ed. *A History of Christianity: Readings in the History of the Church*. Vol. 2, *The Church from the Reformation to the Present*. Englewood Cliffs, N.J.: Prentice-Hall, 1964. Reprint ed. Grand Rapids, Mich.: Baker, 1981.

Murray, John. *The Epistle to the Romans: The English Text with Introduction, Exposition and Notes*. New International Commentary on the New Testament. Grand Rapids, Mich.: Eerdmans, 1959–65.

Nichols, James Hastings. *History of Christianity, 1650–1950: Secularization of the West*. New York: Ronald, 1956.

Oberman, Heiko A. *Luther: Man between God and the Devil*. Translated by Eileen Walliser-Schwarzbart. New Haven: Yale University, 1989.

Pelikan, Jaroslav. *The Christian Tradition: A History of the Development of Doctrine*. Vol. 1, *The Emergence of the Catholic Tradition (100–600)*. Chicago: University of Chicago, 1971.

————. *The Riddle of Roman Catholicism*. Nashville: Abingdon, 1959.

Rahner, Karl. *Schriften zur Theologie*. Vol. 1. Einsiedeln: Benziger, 1964.

Reicke, Bo. *The Epistles of James, Peter, and Jude*. Anchor Bible. Garden City, N.Y.: Doubleday, 1964.

Ridderbos, Herman N. *The Epistle of Paul to the Churches of Galatia*. Translated by Henry Zylstra. New International Commentary on the New Testament. Grand Rapids, Mich.: Eerdmans, 1953.

Ross, Alexander. *The Epistles of James and John*. New International Commentary on the New Testament. Grand Rapids, Mich.: Eerdmans, 1954.

Rupp, Gordon. *Luther's Progress to the Diet of Worms*. London: SCM, 1951; New York: Harper & Row, 1964.

Ryrie, Charles C. *So Great Salvation: What It Means to Believe in Jesus Christ*. Wheaton: Victor, 1989.

Schrenk, Gottlob. *"Dikaiosyne." Theological Dictionary of the New Testament*. Edited by Gerhard Kittel. Translated and edited by Geoffrey W. Bromiley. Vol. 2. Grand Rapids, Mich.: Eerdmans, 1964. Pages 192–210.

Thomas Aquinas. *Nature and Grace: Selections from the "Summa theologica" of Thomas Aquinas*. Edited and translated by A. M. Fairweather. Library of Christian Classics, vol. 11. London: SCM / Philadelphia: Westminster, 1954.

Turretin, Francis. *Institutes of Elenctic Theology*. Translated by George Musgrave Giger. Edited by James T. Dennison Jr. Vols. 1–2. Phillipsburg, N.J.: P & R, 1992–94.

Witsius, Herman. *Sacred Dissertations on What Is Commonly Called the Apostles' Creed*. Translated by Donald Fraser. 2 vols. 1823. Reprint ed. Phillipsburg, N.J.: P & R, 1993.

Latin Glossary

ad infinitum (to infinity, without end), 76

ad nauseam (to a nauseating degree), 76

Agnus Dei (Lamb of God), 104

allocutiones (pronouncements), 31, 120

articulus stantis et cadentis ecclesiae (the article upon which the church stands or falls), 18, 67, 68

assensus (intellectual assent), 75, 78–82

assentire et cooperare (assent to and cooperate with), 125

bene esse (well-being), 180

coram Deo (before the face of God), 96

corde contritus et ore confessus (contrite in heart and having confessed with the mouth), 59

corpus per mixtum (mixed body), 30–31

crux (cross used in executions; pivotal point), 104

de condigno (of condignity), 147

de congruo (of congruity), 147

de merito congrui et condigni (merit of congruence and worthiness), 150

de novo (from the beginning, anew), 55

enchiridion symbolorum (handbook of symbols, creeds), 117

esse (essence, being), 180

ex opere operato (by the work performed), 88

Exsurge Domine (Arise, O Lord), 51, 64

extra (outside of), 119

extra ecclesiam (outside the church), 120

Extra ecclesiam nulla salus (Outside the church there is no salvation), 31, 119–20

extra nos (outside of us), 73, 107, 108

fides viva (vital, living faith), 75, 155

fiducia (cognitive, affective, volitional faith), 75, 80, 82–88, 90

fundamentum (foundation), 121

gratia gratis data (grace freely given), 137

gratia per (propter) Christum (grace through [because of] Christ), 137

gratia praeveniens (prevenient grace), 141

gratis (for nothing), 133, 151

Habere non potest Deum patrem, qui ecclesiam non habet matrem (One cannot have God as one's father if one does not have the church as one's mother), 119

Humani generis (Of the human race), 58, 119

ignorantia (ignorance), 120

initium (beginning), 121

iustificare (justify, declare righteous), 99

iustificatio impii (justify the impious), 73, 97

iustitia alienum (alien righteousness), 107

iustitia extra nos (righteousness outside of or apart from us), 107

massa peccati (mass of sin), 136

meritum de condigno (condign merit), 142

meritum de congruo (congruous merit), 142, 147

Mystici corporis Christi (Of the mystical body of Christ), 58, 119, 120

non cornutum (without horns), 54

notae. See *notitia*

notitia (knowledge), 75–77, 80, 82

Pastor aeternus (Eternal Shepherd), 118

per (by), 122

perditionis (of perdition), 136

per fidem (by faith), 121, 126

per fidem propter Christum (by faith because of Christ), 110

pertinacia (pertinacity), 120

Post tenebras lux (After darkness, light), 17

radix (root), 45, 121

Revoco (I recant), 63

sacrum negotium (holy business), 58

Scala Sancta (Sacred Stairs), 56

semper reformanda (always reforming), 118

simul iustus et peccator (at the same time just and sinner), 102, 102–3, 105, 130

sine qua non (without which, not; something essential), 125

sola (alone), 36, 122, 151, 160, 161

sola fide (faith alone), 18, 19, 21, 30, 36, 42–43, 45, 46, 48, 67, 68, 70, 73, 76, 90, 106, 109, 112, 120, 129, 135, 141, 151, 160, 167, 168, 178–80, 183, 185, 186, 191, 192

sola gratia (grace alone), 109, 135, 142, 151, 192

sola Scriptura (Scripture alone), 21, 41, 63, 67, 135

Soli Deo gloria (Glory to God alone), 192

sub specie boni (under the aspect or form of the good), 187

summa theologica (substance or compendium of theology), 137

tertium quid (something related to two things but distinct from them; something intermediate between two things), 43

Unigenitus Dei Filius (Only begotten Son of God), 58, 63

via media (middle way), 24

votum ecclesiae (unite with the church), 120

votum [ecclesiae] explicitum (an explicit desire to unite [with the church]), 120

votum ecclesiae implicitum (an implicit desire to unite with the church), 120

General Index

accepting Jesus, 29

act of confidence and consolation, faith as an, 90

act of reception and union, faith as an, 88–89

act of refuge, faith as an, 88

Adam, the second, 104–5

affection in *fiducia*, 82, 84, 85

alien righteousness, 107. *See also* imputation

almsgiving, 58

analytical justification, 108–9. *See also* justification

anathema, 127–31, 189

antinomianism, 25, 123, 162, 164, 167, 169

apostasy, 69, 176–83, 184, 189–92. *See also* heresy

Arian heresy, 17–18, 118

assent/*assensus*/assurance. *See under* faith

at the same time just and sinner, 102–3, 105, 130. *See also* imputation

Atlas, 69, 183

atonement, 104, 144, 146. *See also* expiation; propitiation

Augsburg, 62–63

baptism, 41, 57, 75, 122–23. *See also* sacraments

Belgic Confession, 185

betrayal of the gospel. *See under Evangelicals and Catholics Together*

biblical criticism, 24

born-again Christianity, 23

brothers and sisters in Christ, 29–31, 42, 46

Campus Crusade for Christ, 27, 48

canons of Trent. *See* Trent, Council of

carnal Christianity, 25, 168

Carthage, Synod of, 35, 136

Catechism of the Catholic Church, 122–23, 141, 142–43, 149, 150

Catholic Church

Christians outside of, 31, 119–20

evangelical believers in, 186

infallibility of, 46–47, 118

true church according to *Evangelicals and Catholics Together*, 47. *See also* church, the true

See also Catholicism; church

Catholicism

causes of justification according to, 75

faith and works in, 155–71

forensic justification according to, 97

justification according to, 35–36, 117–31

merit and grace in, 135–51

represented in *Evangelicals and Catholics Together*, 27

represented in *Resolutions for Roman Catholic and Evangelical Dialogue*, 46

See also Catholic Church; faith alone; infallibility of Rome; papal declarations, key; scholasticism; Second Vatican Council; Trent Council of

cause

formal, 21, 67, 74

instrumental, 74–75, 88, 122–23

material, 18, 21, 67, 74

causes, Aristotelian categories of, 67, 74

certainty in faith, 81

charismatic movement, 24

formal justification and, 130
infusion, does not exclude, 111, 128
of sin to Christ, 104
Reformation view on, 44
Resolutions for Roman Catholic and Evangelical Dialogue, affirmed by, 45
Trent's canons regarding, 127–31
See also alien righteousness; analytical justification; at the same time just and sinner; *extra nos*, righteousness; imputed grace; imputed righteousness; justification; justification, ground of; legal fiction; merit of Christ; obedience, Christ's perfect; synthetic justification
imputed grace, 105. *See also* imputation
imputed righteousness, 95–113, 168. *See also* imputation
indulgences
definition of, 143
development and application of, 57–60
Ninety-Five Theses and, 61–62
papal declarations concerning, 58
Reformation and, 143–44
treasury of merits and, 142–44
indwelling. *See* Holy Spirit
inerrancy. *See* sola Scriptura
infallibility of Rome, 46–47, 118–20
infallibility of the Bible, 24. *See also* sola Scriptura
infused grace, 105, 146. *See also* infusion
infused righteousness, 117–31. *See also* infusion
infusion, 45, 109, 117–31. *See also* analytical justification; infused grace; inherent righteousness; justification; justification, ground of; material justification; synthetic justification
inherent righteousness
analytical justification and, 109
Calvin on, 101
contradicted by Christ's perfect obedience, 105
doctrine of, 117–31
ground of justification, 108
historical development of doctrine of, 99
justice of God and, 126
material justification and, 130
See also infusion
initial grace of baptism, 57. *See also* grace

International Council on Biblical Inerrancy, 24

James and Paul on faith alone, 161–68
Jehovah's Witnesses, 178
judgment, final, 70
justice of God, 96, 103, 104, 126, 144
justification
agreement on, between Catholics and Evangelicals, 36
analytical and synthetic, 108–9
appropriation of, 19
Augustine on, 99
biblical terminology, meaning of, 99–100
Calvin on, 100–103
Catholic doctrine of, 117–31
Catholicism on, 35–36
causes of, according to Catholicism, 75
central concern over, in the Reformation, 95, 99, 101. *See also under* faith alone; justification, ground of; Reformation
Christ's perfect obedience and, 103–5
concept vs. doctrine of, 98–99, 127, 185
divisive issue in evangelicalism, 26–29, 47–48
evangelical doctrine of, 95–113
Evangelicals and Catholics Together, on, 26–31, 35–37
importance of, 70–73
instrumental cause of, 74–75, 88, 122–23. *See also* cause
justice of God in, 96
Luther's doctrine of, formative influences on, 56–57
McGrath on, 109–13
meaning of, according to the Reformers, 44
of Abraham according to James and Paul, 166
of impious, 70–73, 97, 102
sacraments, by the, 75, 122
sanctification before or after, 98, 110–11, 159–60
second plank of, 144
semantics and, 98–100
Socinian view of, 128
synthetic, 108–9
Trent on, 120–24
waning concern over, 112
works and, 71, 156–60

works of satisfaction and, 145
See also Holy Spirit; justification; regeneration
Satan, 80, 85–86
satisfaction theory of the atonement, 104. See also atonement; expiation; propitiation
satisfaction, works of, 144–46. See also works
Savior, Jesus as, 25, 29, 168–71
scholasticism, 140–41, 142, 150. See also Catholicism
Second Vatican Council, 45. See also Catholicism
semantics and justification, 98–100
semi-Pelagianism, 140–42
simul iustus et peccator. See at the same time just and sinner
sin, 70–71, 96, 136–37, 145, 157–59. See also mortal sin; original sin; venial sin
sincerity, 76
Social Gospel, 22–23
social concern in Evangelicalism, 23
sola fide. See faith alone
sola gratia. See grace alone
sola Scriptura
    erosion of in twentieth-century Evangelicalism, 24
    Evangelicals and Catholics Together, on, 41
    formal cause of the Reformation, 21, 67. See also under cause
    historical origin of Reformation doctrine, 63
    meaning of, 21
    present crisis and, 191
soul freedom, 41
Southern Baptist Convention, 24, 27
Southern Florida Baptist (magazine), 48
state church, 176. See also Catholic Church; church; church, true
subjective theory of value, 86
subjectivism, 76
subsequent grace, 139
sufficient condition, faith as a, 75, 88
superstition, 75–76, 78
syncretism, 76
synergistic work, 146. See also works
synthetic justification, 108–9. See also justification

temporal punishment, merit and, 143. See also eternal punishment
thought, 84–85
tolerance, cultural, 175–76, 177, 180
tower experience, Luther's, 56–57
tradition, 39, 144–45
treasury of merits of Christ and the saints, 58, 61, 142–44. See also merit
Trent, Council of
    basis for shared mission, 185
    canons of, 127–31
    forensic justification in, 97
    grace and merit in, 158
    human merit in, 150
    infused righteousness in, 120–24
    justification by grace in, 35–36
    merit of Christ in, 146
    Resolutions for Roman Catholic and Evangelical Dialogue, on, 45
    semi-Pelagianism and, 140–42
    those outside the Catholic Church in, 120
    works and justification in, 156, 159
    works of satisfaction in, 144
trichotomism, 83
Trinity Evangelical Divinity School, 47
Trinity, the, 18
trust. See fiducia
truth, propositional, 77

Unigenitus Dei Filius. See papal declarations, key
unity, Christian
    between Peter and Paul, 191–92
    Evangelicals and Catholics Together, according to, 28, 29–31, 47
    grounds for, 43, 48
    See also church, the true; Evangelicalism

value, perceived, 86–87
venial sin, 57, 143, 159. See also mortal sin; sin
vicarious atonement. See atonement
volition
    Aquinas on, 139
    cognition and, 82–83
    faith as assent and, 78–79
    fiducia and, 84, 87
    Trent's canons and, 129
    See also faith

Index of Persons

Index of Scripture

R. C. Sproul is the author of *Willing to Believe: The Controversy over Free Will* and *The Last Days according to Jesus,* as well as more than fifty other volumes.

R. C. is founder and chairman of Ligonier Ministries, a teaching ministry that produces Christian educational materials designed to fill the gap between Sunday school and seminary. Beginning as a small study center in Ligonier, Pennsylvania, this ministry moved in 1984 to Orlando, Florida. With a staff of more than fifty people, Ligonier provides laypeople and pastors with substantive materials on theology, church history, Bible study, apologetics, and Christian ethics.

Ligonier's radio program, "Renewing Your Mind," features R. C. and is broadcast nationally, five days a week. Ligonier Ministries produces a monthly periodical, *Tabletalk,* has its own web site (see page 4 for the address), and sponsors several seminars a year, the largest of which is held in Orlando.

R. C. has taught hundreds of thousands of people through books, radio, audio and video tapes, seminars, sermons, seminary classes, and other forums. His goal is to help awaken as many people as possible to the holiness of God in all its fullness. His vision is that believers would apply truth to every sphere of their lives.

Dr. Sproul, a graduate of Westminster College, Pittsburgh Theological Seminary, and the Free University of Amsterdam, is professor of systematic theology and apologetics at Knox Theological Seminary in Fort Lauderdale and is ordained in the Presbyterian Church in America.